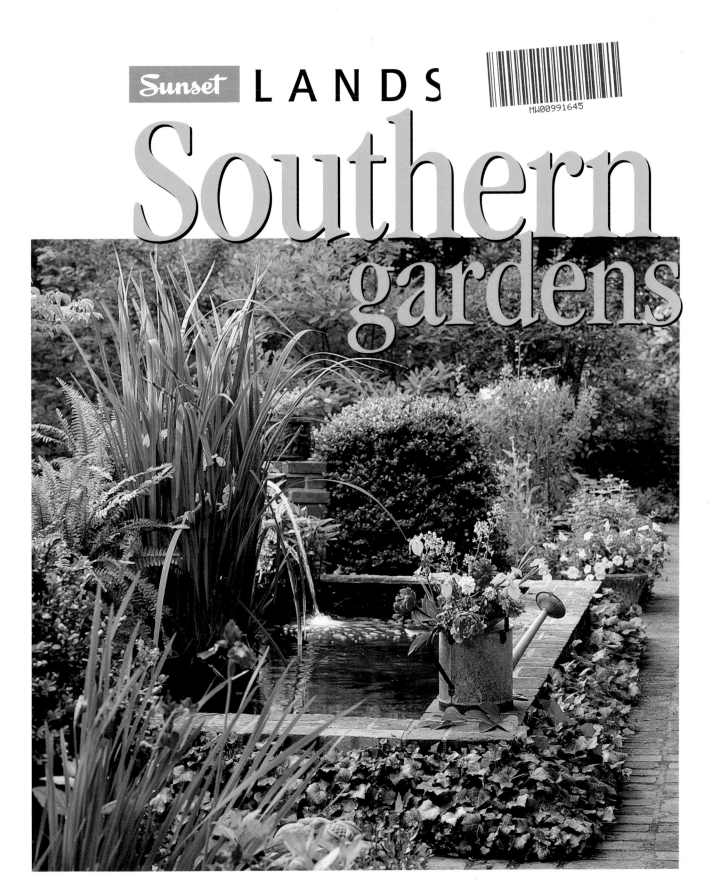

Sunset LANDS

Southern gardens

Edited by Pamela Cornelison and the Editors of Sunset Books

Menlo Park, California

Sunset Books

Vice President, General Manager: Richard A. Smeby
Vice President, Editorial Director: Bob Doyle
Production Director: Lory Day
Operations Director: Rosann Sutherland
Marketing Manager: Linda Barker
Art Director: Vasken Guiragossian
Special Sales: Brad Moses

Staff for this Book

Managing Editor: Pamela Cornelison
Senior Editor & Photo Coordinator: Tom Wilhite
Senior Writers: Philip Edinger, Janet Sanchez
Copy Editor & Indexer: Rebecca LaBrum

Art Director: Gary Hespenheide/Hespenheide Design
Computer Production: Natalie Richmond/Hespenheide Design
Prepress Coordinator: Eligio Hernandez
Production Specialist: Linda M. Bouchard
Production Proofreader: Bridget Neumayr/Hespenheide Design

Cover: Photograph from the Southern Progress
Corporation Photo Collection; cover design by
Vasken Guiragossian

For additional copies of *Landscaping Southern Gardens*
or any other Sunset book, call 1-800-526-5111
or visit us at www.sunset.com.

Paradise Found

If the prospect of landscaping that overgrown yard or clay "hardscape" around your new home seems overwhelming, worry no more. *Landscaping Southern Gardens* can help you create the garden you've always wanted.

Gardeners throughout the South have long been inspired by the Old World—the formal and cottage-style gardens of England, for example, or the courtyard and balcony gardens of France—as well as by the tropical havens of the Americas. These traditions combine with the South's agrarian roots to yield a unique sense of place—the Southern garden style.

Southerners are busy people. Many no longer want to spend weekends pampering a water-greedy lawn or coddling persnickety plants. The lawns that once blanketed suburban landscapes are giving way to functional spaces with easy-care plantings and smaller, more user-friendly lawns better suited to homeowners' tight schedules.

Think about how much time—*and* water—your landscape will need. Even in high-rainfall areas, outdoor watering is sometimes restricted during the hottest months. You may want to consider more water-wise plants for main garden areas, not *just* because they're drought tolerant, but also because most are alluringly carefree.

What is your dream landscape? A free-spirited cottage garden that borders on the rambunctious (pages 40–43)? A tropical landscape complete with native limestone (pages 12–13)? Or a lively composition in Tex-Mex style (pages 36–37)?

Look to this book's first chapter, *Garden Portraits*, for instant inspiration. The second chapter, *Digging In*, covers all aspects of landscape planning, based on sound design principles and practices. *Garden Structures* gives step-by-step directions for building the architectural bones of your landscape—fences, decks, patios, paths, and more. *Plant Palette* provides a tapestry of plant selections, from the best trees for small spaces to ground covers that substitute for lawns. And finally, *Finishing Touches* showcases garden artistry in a range of styles, from formal to whimsical.

Use *Landscaping Southern Gardens* to make your dream a reality— *your* place in which to garden, dine, entertain, and relax.

Contents

6 | Garden Portraits

50 | Digging In

CHAPTER 1

Garden Portraits

Not wholly in the busy world, nor quite beyond it, blooms the garden that I love.

—*Alfred, Lord Tennyson*

Endless Bloom

Tucked away in the verdant Virginia countryside is the ever-evolving garden of a true plant devotee. The personal paradise of owner-designer Donna Hackman, it's a lovingly tended ensemble of native and exotic plants, all arranged to look as if they naturally grew together in just this way.

Stylistically, this is an homage to the English cottage garden: romantic, soft-edged, and always changing. Though there is a basic layout, formal precision isn't foremost. Shrubs give the borders year-round structure, and they're also employed for their variety of forms—upright, horizontal, fountainlike, and weeping, for example. Perennials and annuals establish the cottage mood.

Of course, not everyone has the space or passion for an Eden of these proportions. Still, the insight that Hackman has gained in creating her garden can embolden others to take the plunge, even if on a much smaller scale. To begin with: The will to do the work is more important than the money available. If you want it, *do it*. And in the process, don't hesitate to ask questions. No questions asked, nothing learned—unless the hard way. Don't be afraid of so-called mistakes, including the choice of a plant that languishes or dies; every misstep or setback adds to your knowledge and paves the way for future successes. Don't be afraid to change your plans, either—if you think of a better plant combination or location, take action!

Perhaps the most obvious lesson this garden teaches is the value of planting for all seasons. Creating a spring-flowering garden is easy— but the joy is fleeting. Here, spring and summer flowers are followed by autumn displays of berries and foliage, and then by the beauties of winter: decorative stems and bark, and the blossoms of winter daphne, winter hazel, and Japanese apricot.

FACING PAGE *Native woodland trees firmly anchor the garden to its site, where lavish plantings crowd a carpet of velvety lawn. Prominent in the background is an assortment of hostas, while the base of a venerable oak (foreground) hosts a cool sweep of Spanish bluebells* (Hyacinthoides hispanica).

ABOVE *A lawn-encircled lily pond forms the centerpiece of this extensive landscape. A number of pathways radiate from the pond, leading the visitor into different "outdoor rooms" spread across the garden's three acres.*

BELOW *This scene demonstrates the key to the garden's visual interest: an artful mingling of the contrasting forms and colors of shrubs, trees, perennials, and bulbs in a seemingly natural array.*

RIGHT *A natural rock outcropping provides the perfect spot for a waterfall. Thriving in the moist soil nearby are pink and white Japanese primroses* (Primula japonica) *and blue forget-me-nots* (Myosotis sylvatica).

BELOW *Flowing from the waterfall, a rippling stream winds through a mixed planting prominently featuring a variegated angelica tree (*Aralia elata 'Variegata', left) *and a red-leafed Japanese maple (*Acer palmatum, right).

FACING PAGE, TOP *A concrete birdbath is sheltered by ebullient flowering shrubs. On the right is a white-flowered* Spiraea prunifolia; *on the left, a pink butterfly bush* (Buddleia) *arches above a chartreuse-leafed weigela.*

FACING PAGE, BOTTOM *Early spring in the garden brings forth a soft color contrast between creamy narcissus and lavender* Phlox divaricata.

Old-World Tropics

A Mediterranean-style home with a lush tropical landscape may seem incongruous, but St. Petersburg architect Phil Graham has blended them here in perfect union. The old-world patio flooring and walls serve as an extension of the house, while lush tropical plantings set the rich tone and ambience of the outdoor living space.

Within this sheltered retreat, you'll find areas for entertainment or quiet dining, as well as for observing the area's avian wildlife. In addition, the garden supplies cut flowers and foliage for arrangements to grace the indoors.

Both the terrace and the broad steps leading to it are paved with coquina, a limestone native to this area of Florida composed of crushed shells and coral. Carved coquina also forms the balustrades, and hand-painted blue-and-white Italian tiles showcase the terrace steps.

The plantings are a potpourri of tropical and semi-tropical favorites, including palms, bananas, ferns, and gingers. This densely grouped assortment forms a verdant link between the higher-level house and the ground-level garden. Potted plants and whimsical ornaments nestle in assorted niches amid the tropical luxuriance.

FACING PAGE, INSET *An Italian porcelain pot set in among broad-leafed and lacy foliage captures attention and adds striking detail.*

LEFT *Well-designed terraces and plantings make this patio area both practical and pretty. Pentas, gingers, orchids, and other blooming plants attract butterflies and provide cut flowers.*

ABOVE RIGHT *An ornate wall fountain serves as a focal point, adds the cooling sound of splashing water, and attracts birds to the garden.*

RIGHT *Native limestone steps faced with hand-painted Italian tiles lead to the garden's upper terrace.*

Woodland Haven

Agrove of hardwood trees surrounds Hilda Bolin's property and rustic home in Tennessee. And that's all for the best, since the woodland theme perfectly matches her design style and favorite shade-loving plants.

Bolin feels that plants are a lot like people. "Some are real fussy, while others are easy and just take care of themselves," she says. Knowing not to fight nature, she relies on simplicity of design and a selection of plants that are quite at home on her site—they look as if they could live beyond the garden gate just as easily as within it.

Paths covered with bark chips gently weave around rocks and moss-covered logs, giving visitors a sense of strolling through the woods. Though rocks and logs look as if nature placed them, they were carefully "planted" to recreate a lush glade.

Impatiens planted in the curved stacked-stone beds grace the garden with bright, jewel-toned colors even in deepest shade. Hydrangeas, mahonias, and heavenly bamboo create an intricately textured backdrop, while lacy ferns and broad-leafed hostas lend an air of cool comfort even on the hottest days.

When guests arrive, Bolin makes sure that they are properly greeted at the gate with bouquets of fresh-cut flowers from her garden.

ABOVE RIGHT *This cabin and garden are perfect examples of a landscape that incorporates its natural surroundings. Mulched paths meander past ferns and flowers, moss-covered logs, and native plants before converging at the front door of the cabin.*

NEAR RIGHT *A galvanized watering can springs to life with cut daylilies, Queen Anne's lace, and the handsome veiny foliage of hardy begonias.*

CENTER RIGHT *Above a stacked-stone wall, leatherleaf mahonias and a sweep of red impatiens thrive in the shade of native hardwoods.*

FAR RIGHT *An open gate festooned with cut blossoms of oakleaf hydrangea invites visitors in for a stroll.*

Decades of Change

More than 30 years of renovation have brought welcome change to Jack and Russell Huber's garden in Atlanta. Each day of the journey has been a shared delight for these lifelong gardeners. When they bought the property in 1968, there wasn't much of a garden here. But years of redesign and hard work have transformed a once ordinary outdoor space into the jewel of a retreat it is today.

The pivotal point in renovation was tearing down the old stable they had been using as a greenhouse. Not only did this inspire them to redesign the space, it also encouraged them to create an elegant garden house where the stable once stood. Russell knew they were heading for some big changes when she saw Jack bring home stained-glass windows.

The new structure created an architectural link—a continuity—from garden to home. "It freed some adjoining land and allowed us to build walls, bring in topsoil, make walks, and give [the garden] structure," Jack says. But even with all that, it served mainly to provide a framework—and the beginning of what the garden was to become.

ABOVE *Striking bare trunks and colorful autumn foliage make this Japanese maple a standout year-round. Mondo grass creates a pool of dark green at the tree's base.*

LEFT *Designed to echo the home's architectural style, the garden house brings a sense of continuity to the landscape. With its elegant stained-glass window, it also serves as a handsome focal point. A wooden bench offers a quiet place to sit—and doubles as a temporary holding-station for gardening supplies.*

FACING PAGE, INSET *A stone fish pond (background) serves as a hub for all the garden's paths. This walkway is flanked by daylilies (left) and 'Annabelle' hydrangeas (right).*

From that point on, plantings were allowed to become their own masters—unless they got out of hand. In this iteration of the garden, Louisiana irises punctuate the air from a round fish pond at the junction of the paths. Cheery daylilies and hydrangeas bloom in abundance in summer. Masses of eager ground covers, such as Japanese pachysandra, ajuga, mondo grass, and creeping Jenny, create a plush carpet of green beneath tall hardwoods.

Now, the Hubers have decided it's time to enjoy their garden more and work in it less. By gradually replacing fussier plants, such as hybrid tea roses, with easy-care favorites like Lenten roses *(Helleborus orientalis),* they're encouraging the garden to become more carefree. But, of course, change is nothing new. They've been promoting it for three decades now, and, according to Jack, *that's* not likely to change. "Gardens are always in a state of becoming," he says. "That's good because it energizes and inspires us."

LEFT *The soothing sound of water trickling into the pond from a spillway above adds a magical touch. A moss-covered birdbath repeats the element of water at the opposite end of a path, while masses of low-maintenance ground covers underscore a sweeping view.*

NEAR LEFT *Mantled in Armand clematis, a metal arch over a stone walk frames a floral composition of hydrangeas, daylilies, and impatiens, with a green backdrop of bamboo.*

Weekend Retreat

The owners describe the pretty composition of antique roses, perennials, herbs, and annuals that adorns their weekend home as a modern, Texas-style cottage garden. A well-orchestrated celebration of easy-care choices, it also serves as a test site for new plants as well as a home for old favorites.

It's not by accident that this young Texas garden looks mature—it's by thoughtful design. Horticulturist Bill Welch and landscape architect Nancy Volkman were careful to select unfussy, hard-working plants, such as quick-growing, carefree roses and irises, that would provide structure and add the right palette of colors. Many of the plants were contributed by members of the owners' families. These are easy-care, too, and include pink wood sorrel *(Oxalis crassipes)*, 'Maggie' rose, crinum, Louisiana irises, red carnations, and hardy gladiolus.

The home's architecture dictates the fence type (with a bit of whimsy added in the random placement of pickets and flat-top stakes) and the gable style of gateway arbors. "We wanted a lot of fence space to display flowering vines in addition to roses," Welch says. The fences and arbors not only enclose the garden, but also act as trellises.

Plants here have to be fairly self-reliant, because the owners visit only on weekends. The roses are tough, low-maintenance kinds, the lawn is unthirsty buffalo grass, and the old-fashioned petunias are mainly volunteers that pop up from seeds that fell the previous year.

TOP *This 1906 Victorian cottage is a welcome retreat for weekend getaways. Open vistas and easy-care gardens add to its comfortable charm.*

ABOVE *Fences that enclose gardens on either side of the house carry through the garden's casual theme, and support some favorite climbing roses and vines along the way. A buffalo grass lawn serves as a stage for beds of roses and perennials in blooms of harmonious pastels.*

RIGHT *Texas bluebonnets, pinks, and petunias create splashes of blue, pink, and white beneath a Victorian urn filled with yucca and sedum, while red carnations spill over the path. Gateway arbors echo the architecture of the house.*

Casual Symmetry

Once flanked by foundation shrubs and set on a plain platter of lawn, a 1920s bungalow in Greenville, South Carolina, now boasts a cottage-garden landscape that's perfectly in tune with the home's period charm. But though the effect is relaxed (or even a bit random), an underlying order holds everything together.

Symmetry is the guiding design principle. Sheltered by a stately arbor that repeats the lines of the house eaves, a walkway leads visitors from the gate (painted in warm, welcoming red) to the home's entry. Right-angled pathways of stone and gravel lead through circular plant-ing beds. And within this ordered framework, sumptu-ous assortments of annuals, perennials, vines, herbs, ornamental grasses, ground covers, and shrubs occupy every square inch of space not covered by paths, delight-ing the senses with their varying shapes and colors, in a succession of bloom throughout the year.

Lavish though the garden is, it still doesn't have quite enough planting space for its owner, who freely admits she "wants everything." To accommodate that acquisi-tive urge, containers come to the rescue. Pots of all shapes and sizes fill in whenever the owner needs a mass of green or a spot of seasonal color—liberally adorning

LEFT *In this garden entryway, stepping-stones set in gravel provide access to planting beds overflowing with colorful verbenas, coneflowers, impatiens, and celosias—as well as assorted plants for foliage effect. Variegated miscanthus flanks the door and steps.*

ABOVE *The front garden is chock-full of shrubs and perennials encroaching on an ever-shrinking lawn.*

BELOW *A red gate with a heart-shaped cutout filled with hanging bells invites visitors into the garden. On either side, tall yellow coneflowers (*Rudbeckia nitida *'Herbstsonne') also ring a cheerful welcoming note.*

broad steps, decorating other flat surfaces, even nestling into planting beds. And of course, the containers make it possible to rearrange plantings whenever the mood strikes, without having to dig up a single thing.

Evergreen conifers such as hemlock, spruce, and pine—some in the planting beds, some growing in containers—keep the garden looking alive even during the more barren winter months. The backyard includes a terrace typically crowded with potted ground covers, evergreens, cold-tolerant succulents, and cool-weather annuals. They create a cheerful-looking spot for enjoying the outdoors on mild winter days.

Hilltop Paradise

Though the style of this 1730s saltbox house hails from New England, owner Nancy Gunn Porter built it to look like a centuries-old resident of this wooded hilltop near Little Rock, Arkansas. With the last details of her dream house in place, all she needed was a dreamscape to complete the scene—a garden that would complement the home and link it to the wooded surroundings.

Tipping her hat to the home's architectural roots, Porter created a cottage-style landscape that also has a local naturalistic appeal. Soft pine-straw paths lay the garden's rustic foundation and visually connect it to the woods beyond. Starting with many heirloom plants first grown in Arkansas in the 1730s, like larkspur, old roses, foxgloves, and hollyhocks, Porter then added free-flowering perennials like peonies, pinks, irises, and Shasta daisies to fill out the composition. She relies on this solid foundation of dependable old favorites, but she also enjoys discovering and planting new plants—especially those willing to reseed themselves.

A rustic picket fence frames the site and encloses the exuberant garden. Volunteer seedlings sprout where they may—sometimes even beyond the fenced bounds—reinforcing the casual feel and uniting the garden with the natural landscape.

LEFT *Iceland poppies spark the first seasonal burst of color in this cottage-style garden.*

RIGHT *Here, plants and blooms spill over the fence and scramble toward the woodland beyond. In spring and summer, larkspur, roses, foxglove, butterfly bush, white phlox, cosmos, and verbenas create bursts of color against a backdrop of native evergreens. And in autumn, sugar maples rain golden leaves on purple asters and Mexican bush sage that bloom below.*

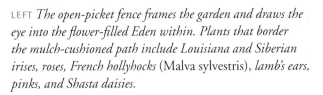

LEFT *The open-picket fence frames the garden and draws the eye into the flower-filled Eden within. Plants that border the mulch-cushioned path include Louisiana and Siberian irises, roses, French hollyhocks* (Malva sylvestris), *lamb's ears, pinks, and Shasta daisies.*

BELOW *These peony plants are more than 50 years old, transplanted to the site from the garden of the owner's mother. Heirloom plants such as old roses and old-fashioned larkspurs share center stage with new and volunteer plants—all in keeping with the Colonial-style home.*

Heaven Scent

Most gardeners would be happy to have a summer-long display of colorful bloom. But in this East Texas spread, Bill and Mary Louise Jobe have focused on something extra: fragrance. To achieve this added dimension, they haven't scoured the world for the rare and exotic; most of the plants are old favorites in this part of the South. The champion of fragrance here is flowering tobacco—not one of the modern hybrids, but the basic tall, white-flowered, night-blooming *Nicotiana alata,* ideal for end-of-day garden enjoyment. Petunias also contribute scent, as do white lilies and 'Ellen Bosanquet' crinum, a Southern classic.

Of course, it's more than sweet perfume that makes this garden so alluring. An inspired mix of heights and textures—and a careful eye toward successive seasons of bloom—form a landscape that is also a visual delight. For height, hollyhocks, Queen Anne's lace, purple-leafed celosia, and spider flower dominate, joined by shrubby salvias 'Anthony Parker' and 'Indigo Spires'. Graceful ornamental grasses with green, purple, and variegated foliage are judiciously placed where their fountainlike forms and wispy textures best provide contrast.

Aside from attention to watering, maintenance is fairly minimal. A few annuals—notably spider flower and flowering tobacco— are cut back after the first bloom flush; new growth furnishes a second flowering later in the season. A number of the annuals were seeded only once; thereafter, volunteer seedlings have returned reliably, year after year.

ABOVE LEFT *Rough-cut stones laid in sinuous curves separate lawn from flower bed. The emphasis is on old-fashioned flowers: tall, white flowering tobacco; 'Laura Bush' petunias in the foreground; and pink and white spider flowers toward the back.*

RIGHT *What the individual blossoms of this flowering tobacco* (Nicotiana sylvestris) *lack in show, they compensate for with their powerful perfume.*

LEFT *Whether viewed from the street or from the shade of the ample veranda, this spacious front garden affords a colorful vista. Pastel and soft colors dominate—a solace from the heat of summer—and many of the flowers are pleasantly fragrant.*

BELOW LEFT *A flowering spike of cat's whiskers* (Orthosiphon aristatus) *shows the prominent stamens that suggest its common name. The bushy, purple-stemmed plants are grown as perennials in frost-free climates and as annuals elsewhere.*

BELOW CENTER *Often overlooked as "just a roadside weed," Queen Anne's lace* (Daucus carota carota) *is a surprisingly effective garden annual. Each flower head forms countless seeds, ensuring a crop of new plants each year.*

BELOW RIGHT *Spider flower* (Cleome hasslerana) *is a favorite annual for summer and fall blooms. In addition to white, flowers come in light to dark shades of purple and crimson on shrubby, spiny-stemmed plants.*

LEFT *Votives glow softly in a candelabra-style sconce on a wall planter, adding a warm ambience to the courtyard. Antique iron corbels support a shelf-table made from native limestone.*

Living Room Alfresco

What better way to enjoy the outdoors than in a courtyard true to its historic Charleston roots? Owner and landscape architect Robert Chesnut captures the classic Southern style in a beautiful "living room" that is quite practical, too.

Walls create the enclosure and give the owners privacy, while tall privet shrubs screen the neighbor's view. Creeping fig and lattice detail soften the walls and make sections of them nearly invisible. Brick flooring in an intricate pattern visually enlarges the space. For Chesnut, the walls and flooring serve his purpose well. "You have to keep the viewer's eye inside the courtyard to create the feeling of a room," he says.

Magic abounds in every detail of the courtyard. The sound of trickling water, the appeal of varying textures, and an inviting place to sit and relax all work together to create a fresh-air room with a spacious yet cozy feel. Much of what makes this design work is the sense of roominess it gives. An example is the curved lattice panel that contains a wall fountain spouting water into a cistern below. "To give the illusion of more space and to make the wall behind the fountain appear open, I painted the stucco behind the lattice black," Chesnut says. By repeating architectural details such as the curved latticework and choosing furnishings scaled to the room, he maintains a feeling of openness. Another trick lies in the brick flooring. He uses a modified herringbone pattern, which emphasizes diagonal lines, to make the courtyard seem larger.

The final challenge for Chesnut was in planning a comfortable place to sit and dine without using too much precious space or blocking traffic flow in the courtyard. The solution came in adding comfortable chairs that are in perfect scale with the room, and a handsome stone shelf that serves as a table.

LEFT *The courtyard is a long, narrow L shape—but brick flooring laid in a diagonal pattern, small-scale fountain, vertical plantings, and shallow shelf-table give it a spacious feel.*

NEAR LEFT *The fountain is made of curves: the arched shapes of the lattice backing and stucco edging are repeated in the water basin. For a sense of space beyond the lattice, the wall behind the fountain was painted black.*

Sweet Legacy

To see this well-ordered Louisiana landscape now, awash in lavish colors and textures, you'd never guess it once was a field of sugarcane. It took the vision of the designer and owner, Michael Hopping, to see beyond the original—a flat plot on the banks of the Mississippi, surrounding an old overseer's cottage—and realize its potential.

Though filled with plants, the landscape feels uncrowded, thanks to the brick-edged gravel pathways that divide it into individual areas. In a design idea borrowed from England, clipped boxwoods anchor the garden's corners and add formal contrast. Differing sizes and shapes keep things interesting: there are hollyhocks for vertical emphasis, lily-of-the-Nile for fountainlike foliage, bold-leafed callas and bananas for tropical effect, and old-fashioned flowers like poppies and phlox for informal charm.

Throughout the garden, metal sculptures, stone urns, and recycled pieces from the property's past provide contrast to the plantings. The focal point is a surprising relic from yesteryear: a tin-roofed 1850s privy, now a toolshed! As the garden's tallest structure, it gains in visual importance in this pancake-flat terrain.

ABOVE *Two chairs strategically placed in the shade invite a pause to enjoy the sound of the garden's centerpiece: a gently splashing fountain made from a sugar kettle that was saved from the property's previous life as a sugarcane plantation.*

RIGHT *Taking off in several directions from the kettle-fountain, gravel pathways lead through well-ordered beds of plants that are perfectly adapted to this steamy Louisiana climate.*

Sweet Legacy

ABOVE *A simply wrought metal rooster stands guard from his perch in a hedge of clipped boxwood, while clumps of sculptural white calla lilies reach for the sky.*

RIGHT *Though the plantings are informal and exuberant, they're encased in neat beds formed by a grid of straight pathways. A rose arbor fashioned from lengths of iron tubing—like two intersecting croquet wickets—frames a view of the garden from the front gate.*

FACING PAGE, INSET *A rustic toolshed— an antique structure rescued from an even more utilitarian past—becomes a focal point when framed by gateposts and flanked by potted boxwoods. Its plain surface forms a neutral backdrop for a French olive jar and statuesque hollyhocks.*

RIGHT *The garden's colorful flowers and varied foliage greens are surprisingly complementary to the purple hue of the house. A south-of-the-border mood is established by vivid, bright colors as well as by characteristic plants like the prickly pear cactus.*

BELOW *This wrought-iron gate opens from a small parking area into a series of garden "rooms" hidden behind the limestone wall.*

FACING PAGE, TOP *A hand-painted Mexican bowl finds a new life as a festive birdbath.*

FACING PAGE, BOTTOM *A folk-art Madonna in a rustic niche is one of this garden's many ornaments fashioned by local artisans.*

Purple Reign

Whoever coined the phrase "shrinking violet" never saw this Austin, Texas, garden. The vivid purple house sets the tone and provides the backdrop for a riot of color. Blossoms in vibrant hues of red, yellow, orange, and (of course) purple mingle in the planting beds, while foliage in varied shades of green keeps bold colors from clashing. What could have been an eye-assaulting collision of color is, instead, a fiesta landscape that celebrates owner Lucinda Hutson's fondness for Mexican culture—and brings back happy memories of her El Paso childhood. Purple was her grandmother's favorite color, in everything she wore and owned.

To make the most of limited space, the front yard, formerly open to the street, has been divided by a wall of stacked Texas limestone. It's now two areas: a parking court or public area at the front of the wall, and a private space at the side and to the rear of the wall that's entered through a tall gate adorned with vines overhead. The garden was sectioned into a series of spaces or vignettes—each its own landscape in scale—that provide areas for day-to-day outdoor living and closely link home and garden. Indoor and outdoor spaces flow into each other, encouraging guests to move from house to yard and back again. With an emphasis on using native Texas elements in a Mexican style, each space combines not only colorful flowers from both sides of the border, but also culinary herbs to satisfy another of the owner's passions—regional cooking. Carefully chosen pieces of folk art round out the Tex-Mex picture. "My garden is such a personal place, filled with special things my friends have made and memories of my travels," Hutson says. "They are as important to the garden as the flowers and herbs."

The overall effect of the garden is both artful and jubilant, a landscape that conveys a love of intense color and cultural styles. For Hutson, much of the joy of growing her garden is in sharing its beauty and plants (cuttings) with neighbors who just stop in. "My garden is starting to stretch down the street, and that's really fun," she says.

Knot Squared

The motivation for creating this rectangular easy-care parterre was the Birmingham owner's desire for a low-maintenance planting—one that would replace a temperamental rose garden that demanded too much time. Combining beauty with utility, designer Mary Zahl fashioned a knot garden that suited the owner's needs and the home's formal architecture. The space also doubles as a welcoming retreat—a place to sit, relax, and enjoy the view.

The home's site is terraced, with the knot garden located on a lower level. Because it is viewed from the upper terraces, the garden needs to look good from the areas above. A sundial creates a focal point in the center, surrounded by a knot of sheared Japanese holly and abelia hedges that provide year-round interest and require little care. Flower borders flank the sides with seasonal color, while small boxwoods in elevated containers anchor corners and beds. "It's a way of giving impact," Zahl says of the potted evergreens. "A small boxwood in a pot has a similar or greater impact than a large one in the ground." Planting an evergreen like boxwood in a container also makes the plant portable and easy to move to different areas of the site.

Zahl repeated materials such as weathered brick and stone used elsewhere on the property to "age" the new garden and connect it with the older style of the house.

BELOW LEFT AND BELOW *A bank of 'Nellie R. Stevens' holly shrubs helps to define the space and make it feel roomy yet cozy. The evergreens planted throughout keep formal lines in place and add year-round appeal. The borders bloom with bursts of ever-changing color through the seasons.*

LEFT *Boxwoods in containers emphasize the garden's shape and formal style. Planting these evergreen shrubs in pots and elevating them increases their impact in the setting.*

RIGHT *A graceful, country-style wooden gate opens on a timber pathway leading directly to one of many garden "rooms" in this imaginative landscape.*

FAR RIGHT *Semicircles of hedged boxwood embrace a circular bed planted with towering white foxgloves and surrounded by a flagstone path. Arbors stand sentinel on either side of the garden, the right-hand one smothered in a froth of white rose blossoms.*

BELOW *An opening in a low brick wall reveals a lawn backed by a stylized temple made from rustic logs of eastern red cedar.*

Esprit Classic

Ryan Gainey will be the first to say his garden is built on older bones. Decades ago, this plot in Decatur, Georgia, was the site of a nursery specializing in cut flowers and potted plants. But instead of completely revamping his inherited landscape, Gainey had the vision to retain the best of it, then gradually develop his own design for the rest. Though today's garden shows no outward signs of a utilitarian past, the original footprint actually forms its foundation. Where greenhouses once stood, gardens now grow. The transformation from nursery planting to pleasure garden is a tribute to Gainey's artistic eye and horticultural sophistication.

The total landscape is now divided into a succession of garden "rooms" arranged in an architectural grid. Paths form the central axis in most of the rooms and also run in straight lines between rooms. Each area is surrounded by trellises, hedges, or house walls; within each room, shrubs and hedges impose a general sense of order, but flowering and foliage plants steal the show as they mingle in seemingly casual abandon. This thoughtfully balanced combination of opposing elements—structure and informality—lends a special charm. "All the rooms are expressions of my love for classical garden design, but they are expressed in a cottage-garden setting," says Gainey.

This exuberant garden is much more than just a floral showcase, though. It's a pleasure for all seasons, thanks to combinations of plants chosen with an eye toward color, texture, form, and the relationship of all these to the architectural elements. The result is peaceful, inspiring, educational—and simply lovely.

Garden Portraits

RIGHT *Clipped boxwood hedges set on the diagonal to bed margins give a sense of organization to the loosely structured plantings, while cylinders of yew offer vertical accents. Logs span the area, giving vining plants a place to latch on.*

FACING PAGE, INSET *Summer-flowering* Spiraea japonica—*shown here in companionable beauty with a purple-flowered clematis—is one of the garden's never-fail flowering shrubs.*

BELOW *A tower made of black locust wood and roofed with tin offers a vantage point for a panoramic view of the garden.*

Garden Pool Room

Sometimes it takes more than a garden makeover to give life to a tired landscape design. Originally, this small yard in Dallas was a pool enclosed in an exposed-aggregate deck accessed by sliding glass doors—a piece of period style whose era had passed unlamented. Now, with some cosmetic retooling to house and paving and an updated design, the space is a gem of a garden "room."

To start the transformation, architect Dale Selzer replaced the dated sliding glass panels with a series of heavy-framed French doors. The existing window frames and cantilevered arbor were painted gray to match the new doors and harmonize with the rest of the house. For the pool deck, flagstone was landscape architect Naud Burnett's paving of choice; in blended shades of gray, green, and tan, it complements the mottled tones of the brick walls. Light green plaster was used for the pool's base and coping.

"The area is so small, you need neutral colors to make it seem as big as possible," Burnett says. The colors also "fade" structures into the background, creating a perfect stage for the scene of lush plantings.

Dogwoods, 'Savannah' holly, Japanese maple, live oaks, and yaupons are the garden's foundation, while Chinese hibiscus and caladiums offer splashes of seasonal color both in the ground and in containers.

LEFT AND FACING PAGE, TOP *A simple border of green and white caladiums softens the pool's stone edging and complements its Caribbean blue water. Enclosed by house, garden walls, and plentiful greenery, the inviting pool and patio are an alfresco extension of the home's living space.*

FACING PAGE, BOTTOM LEFT *Careful, well-planned color choices unite paving, painted surfaces, and patio furnishings. The warm-hued flagstones link the paving to existing brick walls.*

FACING PAGE, INSET *Stepping-stones surrounded by greenery blur the distinction between pavement and plantings while allowing easy access into a seating alcove and planting beds.*

BELOW *Steel gray river rock looks like a decorative touch, but it actually serves a practical purpose. The rock conceals a drain between house and pool deck that keeps runoff out of the pool.*

Elegant Simplicity

The view from a third-story window shows off the simple yet elegant design of this classic garden in Georgia. Liz Tedder, the designer and owner, favors clean lines and vistas, as well as lush border plantings that endure throughout the seasons.

Perennials, shrubs, and seasonal annuals create the parallel mixed borders that extend 100 feet out from a terrace on the home's south side. A green carpet of tall fescue, a variety selected for its cool-season color and tolerance of sun or shade, serves as a walkway between the borders and as a backdrop for the seasonal blooms. A hexagonal gazebo—the garden's handsome focal point—is directly in line with the window that affords the bird's-eye view of the garden. White picket fences and Yoshino flowering cherries at the back of each planting bed hold the design's lines, bring order to free-flowering plants in borders, and direct the eye to the gazebo.

A look back toward the house from the gazebo makes it obvious that Tedder has a passion for crisp lines and uncluttered views. Repetition of color and materials, attention to scale, and a composition of perfect symmetry give a feeling of continuity and easy flow. The terrace and garden edgings repeat the materials and color of the twin chimneys, while the fences and gazebo mirror those of the house.

The garden furnishes plenty of cut flowers from a well-chosen palette of plants. And except in the coldest part of the winter, blooms are abundant year-round. Tedder divides and thins overcrowded perennials every four to five years to keep plants in top bloom. When she digs the perennials, she also takes time to rework the mixed borders. Plantings include flowering cherries, pansies, tulips, irises, peonies, and roses in spring; daylilies, balloon flowers, phlox, and coneflowers in summer; salvias and asters in autumn; and pansies in winter. Reseeding annuals, such as love-in-a-mist and dame's rocket *(Hesperis matronalis),* readily fill any gaps in the bloom cycle.

ABOVE *Cut flowers from the garden change ordinary watering cans into pretty vases. Comfortable wicker chairs add to the gazebo's cozy feel.*

LEFT *Open to breezes that carry floral scents from the garden, this gazebo serves in grand style as a sitting room and garden focal point.*

FACING PAGE *A birds-eye view from upstairs showcases the symmetry of this formal garden. A centered carpet of lawn displays brick-edged flower beds to perfect advantage. White picket fences reinforce the classic look and keep the viewer's eye moving toward the gazebo.*

ABOVE *Dame's rocket is a favorite annual in this mixed border, where its volunteer seedlings fill gaps between perennial bloomers. Its lavender-pink flowers blend nicely with pansies and 'Pink Meidiland' shrub roses.*

RIGHT *Luscious peony blooms star in the spring garden, with pink 'Sarah Bernhardt' taking center stage in this border. When these divas of spring finish blooming, a supporting cast of flowering perennials and annuals extends the show in scenes of colorful bloom.*

FACING PAGE, INSET *A view from the cozy gazebo to the house clearly shows the rhythm and scale of this garden's balanced design. The brick landing and edging pick up the color of the twin chimneys, while the gazebo and fences repeat the color of the house.*

From Rough Sketch to Final Plan

A. *Planting a hedge on the hill along the street will help block the wind as well as traffic noise.*

B. *A shade garden is suitable for this microclimate on the north side of the house.*

C. *A fountain placed here can be seen from inside the house as well as from the patio.*

D. *This south-facing spot offers plenty of sun for a vegetable or cutting garden.*

E. *A smaller lawn means less watering, feeding, and mowing.*

F. *A children's play area is sited where it can be safely supervised from both patio and house.*

G. *The patio is shaded from the hot sun by an arbor.*

H. *Part of the driveway is replaced with a hedge for screening.*

I. *A new walkway is added from the driveway to the front door.*

J. *Trees in the front yard will help block wind and reduce the area of high-maintenance lawn.*

K. *A little getaway is located far from the house.*

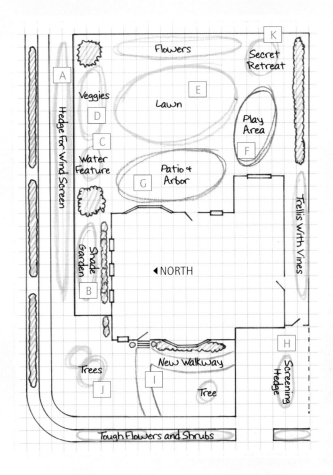

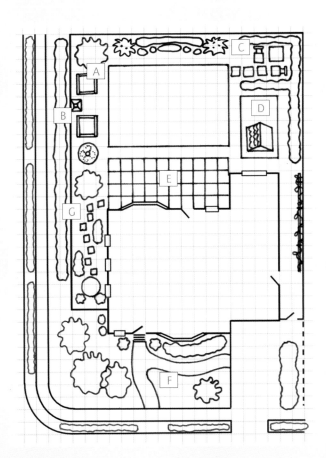

Now that you've narrowed down possible locations for the new elements, you're ready to develop the final plan. To get a better grasp of the layout and to feel more confident about the best place for each new feature, you may want to mock up the design on your property using stakes, strings, or markings (chalk outlines, for instance; see page 79).

A. *Raised beds are ideal for growing herbs and vegetables.*

B. *The compost bin is convenient to vegetable and herb beds, lawn, and kitchen, where much of the raw material for compost is produced.*

C. *For the retreat, a continuation of the existing hedge will give a sense of enclosure, and a couple of chairs and a small table will make the space comfortable.*

D. *A sandbox and playhouse make an inviting play area for the kids.*

E. *A low wooden patio with an arbor adjoins the house.*

F. *The front walkway has a graceful curve.*

G. *Stepping-stones lead from the patio into the shade garden.*

Design Basics and Tricks

Whatever garden style you choose, your plan will be more successful if you follow some of the simple guidelines that landscape professionals use. In a well-designed garden, no single structure or feature is completely dominant. Rather, all the parts work together to establish a sense of *unity*, ensuring that the garden is seen as a beautiful whole rather than a hodgepodge of disparate elements. Make sure that all the components—structures, planting beds, borders, water features—are in *proportion* to each other and in *scale* with the size of your house and property. With *repetition* of plants, colors, and materials, you can bring *rhythm* and *emphasis* to the design. And you can create a feeling of *harmony* and *balance* by combining simple lines and forms with a variety of plants and structural materials.

In addition to these basic principles, professionals employ an assortment of tricks to overcome typical challenges or simply to create a more attractive and livable garden. To enlarge the space visually and integrate it more closely with the surroundings, *borrow scenery* by bringing views from beyond the garden's boundaries into the design. For small spaces in particular, you can also make the area seem larger by adding vertical elements that divide it into a series of "rooms." In a small or narrow garden, *emphasize diagonal lines* to make the space look larger. For an air of mystery and discovery, *conceal parts of the garden;* you might place a bubbling fountain around a bend in a path, so that visitors go in search of the sound. And to add drama, *place a large plant or object in a small space.*

You can learn a lot from other gardens. Visit as many in person as you can, and study the photographs you find in magazines and throughout this book. Try to relate the key elements you notice to the design principles illustrated here. Then keep them in mind as you plan your own garden.

FACING PAGE, LEFT Proportion *refers to the way elements fit the space and each other. The garden as a whole should also be in scale with the size of the house and property.*

FACING PAGE, RIGHT Symmetry, *most often employed in formal garden designs, exists when matching elements are balanced on either side of a central axis. A pleasing effect can also be achieved with asymmetry, when elements around the axis are different.*

ABOVE *A* focal point *is a "standout" plant, structure, or other object, located to attract attention and draw in the observer.*

ABOVE RIGHT Simplicity *is the result of restraint. Unfussy compositions are inviting and calming, but a garden that has too many different elements— contrasting forms, textures, and colors— may feel overwhelming and chaotic.*

RIGHT Rhythm *can be attained through repeated elements, such as matching colorful blooms or plants of similar shape. It creates a satisfying sense of order and unity of theme and can help lead your eye through the space.*

BELOW *An* accent *contrasts boldly with its surroundings, enlivening a composition by adding variety and depth.*

A

Watering Systems

An irrigation system should fit the lay of your land and the arrangement of your plants. It should suit your schedule, too: be careful not to choose a system that demands more time than you have to spend. A wealth of equipment is available to help you water your garden efficiently, even when you're busy or out of town.

Hose-end Sprinklers

These come in a variety of forms, from impulse sprinklers that can cover hundreds of square feet to small bubblers ideal for watering shrubs or containers.

Choose models with a spray pattern that matches the areas you'll be watering. If you have clay soil or sloping ground that is slow to absorb water, select types that steadily apply low volumes over long periods to avoid wasteful runoff. The downside of hose-end sprinklers is that you have to move them around by hand to cover large areas. They also deliver water unevenly; some areas get wetter than others. To get an idea of the delivery rate and distribution pattern, place five identical, straight-sided cups randomly in the coverage area, run the sprinkler for 15 to 30 minutes, and then measure the contents of each cup. The amount of water—and where it accumulated—will give you an idea of how long to run the sprinklers and how to move them so that coverage patterns overlap and all the plants are watered evenly.

Soaker Hoses

Soaker hoses offer one of the simplest and least expensive ways to water. Unlike a complete drip or sprinkler system, they attach to hose bibs quickly and with little fuss. Of the two types available, one applies a fine spray, the other small droplets. Both are generally sold in 50- and 100-foot lengths.

In spray types, perforated plastic emits water from uniform holes drilled along one side. The hose can be used face down, so water goes directly into the soil, or turned face up for broader coverage.

With ooze tubing, or "leaky hose," water seeps out of tiny pores. A filter in the nozzle is required to prevent clogging, and water is applied slowly and steadily along the entire length of the hose. If you don't use a pressure regulator, turn on the water until it seeps out of the pores. If you see pinhole sprays, reduce the pressure. For large beds, run the hose out in rows spaced 2 to 3 feet apart. To keep it from being an eyesore, cover it with mulch or bury it 2 to 6 inches deep.

Drip Irrigation

For trees, shrubs, flowers, and vegetables, drip irrigation is the most efficient way to get water down to the

A. Drip hose with factory-drilled holes lets water slowly drizzle out.

B. Water from emitter line spreads slowly through soil to moisten plant roots.

C. Porous polyvinyl tubing soaks soil at high pressure; at low pressure, water seeps.

D. Delivery tubes for irrigation systems include (left to right) ½-inch-diameter tube, spaghetti tube, and soaker tubes of different sizes.

E. Other components of an irrigation system are (left to right) emitters, mini-sprinklers, and connection to the water source and timer, including a Y-shaped filter and pressure regulator.

D

E

roots. Water is applied slowly, so it can be absorbed without runoff—and it goes directly where it's needed, so you use less (and minimize weed growth, too).

Drip irrigation systems are surprisingly easy to install. The key is good planning and design. Start with a detailed drawing of the garden, showing the positions and spacing of plants, and learn each plant's water needs: is it drought tolerant or does it require frequent irrigation? If you're starting a new garden, group the plants according to their water needs. Rough out your plan on paper and take it to an irrigation contractor for some expert help with the design and maintenance of your self-installed system.

Sprinkler Systems

Traditionally used for watering lawns, underground pipe systems with risers for sprinkler heads offer the best way to water medium-size to large lawns and low-growing ground covers.

You may need to divide your sprinkler system into several circuits, each serving only part of the lawn or garden and operated by its own valve. Then you can water each circuit separately, as needed. Established shrubs, for instance, may need watering only every 10 to 14 days; lawns may require a thorough soaking twice a week.

Automated Irrigation

An automatic system, operated with either electric or manual timers (see below), is the most efficient way to water. Controllers capable of daily multiple cycles reduce runoff, which occurs when water is applied faster than the soil can absorb it. If you have this problem, set a repeat cycle to operate the sprinklers for 10 to 15 minutes at, for example, 4, 5, and 6 A.M.

Dual- or multiple-program controllers let you water a lawn more frequently than you do ground covers, shrubs, and trees.

Timers

To water your garden (or parts of it) for a set amount of time, install an electric-powered or manual timer. Both types can be set up to run a drip system, a sprinkler system, or any common watering device, such as a hose-end sprinkler.

Electric timers are the more expensive kind; they're either battery powered or require an outlet. The controls vary, ranging from pretty straightforward to very complex; for instance, you can set up circuits that water different parts of your yard at different intervals for different time periods. A word of caution: If a professional installs

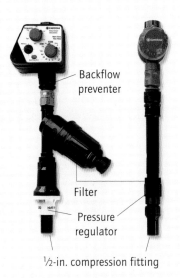

Backflow preventer

Filter

Pressure regulator

½-in. compression fitting

the system for you, be sure you receive the printed instructions for resetting the controls (which you'll need to do if, for instance, a power failure wipes out the timer's settings).

Manual timers are not as convenient as automatic types, since you must actually walk out to the garden and turn them on, but they're less prone to breakage and have automatic shut-off valves that stop the water when the time is up—so there's less risk of overwatering all or part of the garden.

Timers are installed between the faucet and any other system components, including backflow preventers, filters, and pressure regulators.

Flooring the Outdoor Room

Think of your garden as an outdoor room that needs a floor, ceiling, and walls to give it form and function. For all these "surfaces," you have a variety of choices.

The most noticeable part of the garden "room" is the "floor," which may include a lawn, planting areas, a pathway, a patio or deck, or even a pool. Aside from serving different functional purposes, garden floors can modify the climate: a large concrete slab will reflect the sun's heat, while dark pavement such as asphalt will collect heat during the day, then release it at night. A lush ground cover, in contrast, will reduce the air temperature around it by several degrees. Living garden floors can provide an uninterrupted carpet of green foliage or an elaborate mosaic of brightly colored flowers. They also play a protective role—shielding the soil from wind and too much sun, and knitting it together to prevent erosion.

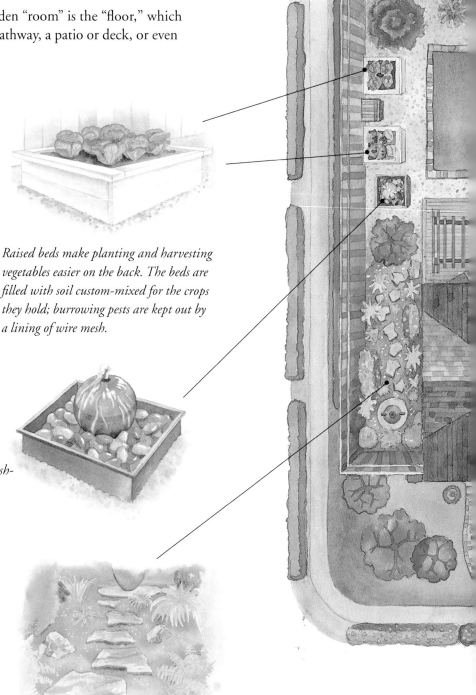

Raised beds make planting and harvesting vegetables easier on the back. The beds are filled with soil custom-mixed for the crops they hold; burrowing pests are kept out by a lining of wire mesh.

A recirculating fountain in a contemporary style pleases both eyes and ears, creating a focal point while enhancing the garden with the soothing murmur of water splashing onto stones.

Stepping-stones lead through lush plantings on the shady side of the house. The path's end—visible from indoors as well—is a perfect spot for displaying a favorite art object.

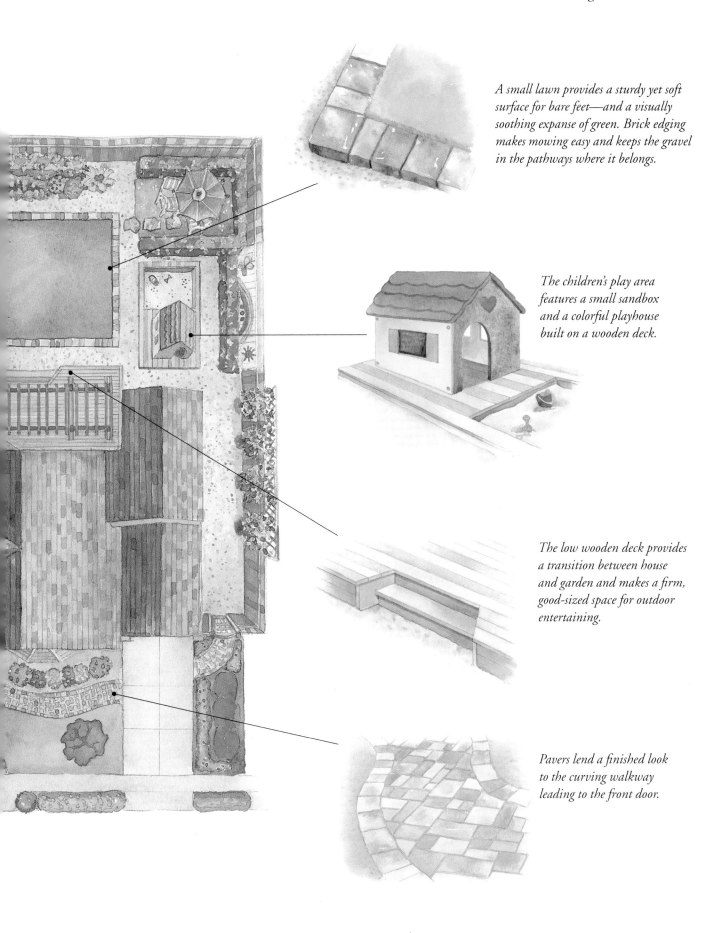

A small lawn provides a sturdy yet soft surface for bare feet—and a visually soothing expanse of green. Brick edging makes mowing easy and keeps the gravel in the pathways where it belongs.

The children's play area features a small sandbox and a colorful playhouse built on a wooden deck.

The low wooden deck provides a transition between house and garden and makes a firm, good-sized space for outdoor entertaining.

Pavers lend a finished look to the curving walkway leading to the front door.

Enclosing the Outdoor Room

The "walls" of a garden define the space and offer whatever degree of privacy you desire. Fences, hedges, concrete or brick walls, small trees and large shrubs—all can shield your garden from the street or neighbors, and block wind, sun, or unsightly views. The "ceiling" may simply be the bright blue sky or a canopy of trees; or it may come from an arbor, a pergola, or even an umbrella or fabric awning. Gardens often have several different ceilings, each creating a different feel. A dining area, for example, benefits from overhead shade, while an herb bed needs maximum exposure to sunshine.

A fence defines the backyard's boundaries. Here, a tall hedge serves as an additional wind screen and noise barrier; it helps to block undesirable views, as well.

An overhead arbor constructed as part of the deck offers shelter from hot sun and a sturdy support for vines.

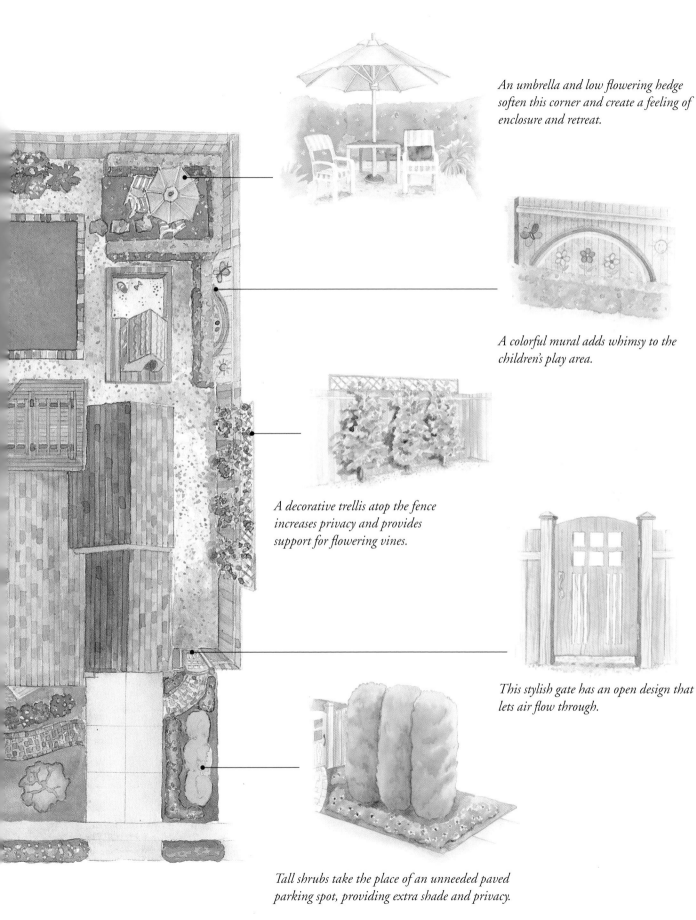

An umbrella and low flowering hedge soften this corner and create a feeling of enclosure and retreat.

A colorful mural adds whimsy to the children's play area.

A decorative trellis atop the fence increases privacy and provides support for flowering vines.

This stylish gate has an open design that lets air flow through.

Tall shrubs take the place of an unneeded paved parking spot, providing extra shade and privacy.

Front Yards

As the most visible part of your property, your front yard should enhance your home's architectural style and offer a warm welcome to visitors—yet still maintain a degree of privacy. In a well-planned front garden, the plantings are carefully chosen, including evergreens (to give structure and keep the yard looking lush year-round) as well as an assortment of deciduous and flowering plants to mark the passing seasons. Within these guidelines, there's room for enormous variety: you might have a formal lawn edged with clipped foundation shrubs, a casual cottage garden bursting with exuberant color, or a serene woodland composition of trees, ferns, and boulders.

In any landscape, be sure the path to the front door is both easy to find and well lit at night. And through-out the yard, aim for walkways that are wide enough to let people walk side by side rather than single file.

ABOVE *Like open arms, curving brick walls welcome visitors while holding back the slope. The warm red color picks up the tones of the roof, while the soft gray of the drive echoes the painted brick of the house walls.*

LEFT *Winding through flowery mounds, a curving path leads to a gracious entry featuring wrought-iron chairs and a small table. Even if it's not frequently used, the furniture suggests welcome and repose.*

TOP RIGHT *This cheerful stand of sunflowers makes an innovative, open-textured privacy screen for a front yard. Evergreen shrubs like nandina or abelia could be used to create a similar but more permanent effect.*

ABOVE *A tropical paradise can replace conventional lawns in the southernmost parts of Florida and Texas, where palms, bromeliads, and other exotic plants thrive in the year-round warmth.*

LEFT *A stone wall topped with lush green shrubs and fronted by benches meets both public and private needs.*

Side Yards

The typical side yard may be only a few feet wide and quite shady, but there's often just enough room for an interesting little garden. A simple solution is to install stepping-stones and low-growing, shade-tolerant ground covers. If unattractive block walls separate your side yard from your neighbor's, secure planter boxes along the top and fill them with cascading plants. You might also create an espalier on a trellis or on wires attached to the wall or fence. A neglected fence out of public view might be just the spot to hang a collection of found art or let your kids paint a mural. And a series of arching trellises covered with vines will create a green roof over your side yard and turn it into a pleasant, secluded corridor.

In a more functional vein, you can locate your compost bin here or use the space to store extra pots, watering cans, and potting soil. Or pave the area with bricks and build a handsome "recycling center": covered shelves where metal, glass, and paper can be neatly kept until recycling day.

TOP RIGHT *This cedar pergola has an open design that admits enough sunlight for plants to thrive along the side of the house.*

RIGHT *A woodland scene unfolds in this cool green passage between house and fence. Hydrangeas and impatiens bloom happily in the dappled shade.*

Driveways

Though it's one of the most visible features of many properties, the driveway is often overlooked in its potential for enhancing a site. Remember that it's really part of your home's entry—so if parking is accessible and the walk to the house is pleasant, you've extended a gracious welcome before you even open the door.

If you're designing a new driveway and parking area, think carefully about how many parking spots you need. Not enough space means constant shuffling, but pave too much and your yard may resemble a valet lot. Consider adding a handsome wall or a row of tall shrubs to screen the parking area.

Narrow Spaces

The poor cousin of the neglected driveway is that parched ribbon of unclaimed territory right out front between sidewalk and street. Planting trees in such an area requires careful consideration: some have invasive roots that can buckle concrete sidewalks, and others grow too tall to fit beneath overhead power lines. To dress up a curbside, experiment with a variety of rugged perennials, bulbs, and small shrubs that are unfussy about soil and don't need extra water. Not everything you choose will thrive, but over time you can repeat successful choices until you have just the right mix of beauty and vigor.

The driveway itself doesn't have to be simply a gray slab of poured concrete. To dress up existing concrete, have it stained, bonded, or top-coated in a color and finish that will complement your home. Or replace it with stone pavers, bricks, cobblestones—even gravel. You can also add a center strip of contrasting material, such as crushed rock or low-growing plants, or even opt for a checkerboard pattern of concrete pads alternating with squares of grass, ground cover, or gravel.

To give your visitors a lovely first impression as they pull into the drive, consider softening the edges with beds of shrubs or colorful flowers—always making sure there's plenty of clearance for getting out of the car.

TOP RIGHT *Welcoming by design, this compact front yard features a gravel parking court that opens onto a flagstone walk. A comfortable bench offers an appealing place to pause.*

ABOVE *Neat as a pin, the clipped hedges and formal espaliers enclosing this narrow parking area perfectly match the tailored style of the house.*

ABOVE *This formal yet inviting composition includes a rectangular bed edged in clipped shrubs. A bench snuggled beneath an arbor is the perfect vantage point for viewing the garden's focal point: a lovely fountain that spills into a small pond.*

LEFT *Raised beds surrounded by a patio of flagstone set in decomposed granite give this sunny backyard a crisp, distinctive look.*

FACING PAGE, TOP *A circular lawn and brick patio make this formerly rectangular backyard seem far more expansive and calming.*

FACING PAGE, CENTER *A naturalistic waterfall is set into a lushly planted wooded slope. Sentinel grasses at the path's beginning add a touch of formality.*

FACING PAGE, BOTTOM *In drier regions of the South, where drought-tolerant trees, shrubs, and perennials are smart choices, a small lawn can have a big impact.*

Backyards

The front yard is the public face of your property—but out back, you can let your hair down and use the space pretty much as you please. Instead of the traditional lawn, perhaps you'd like mulched paths winding among an assortment of native plants. Maybe your site lends itself to the illusion of a waterway, with a series of small falls cascading from the highest point down to a lushly planted pond. Do you want a serene retreat where you can sit quietly in the dappled shade—or an outdoor gathering place with a patio, pool, and comfortable chairs around a fireplace? Do you plan to display a collection of delicate specimen plants, or do you envision an inviting playground for kids and pets?

As you plan your backyard, think of it as an extension of your home, and keep in mind how it will look from inside—in general, houses have more doors and windows opening to the back. This private area is like another living room, so make it a place you, your family, and guests will want to be. The main thing is to have an overall concept in mind that you'll enjoy seeing through. And don't worry if the details change; just enjoy the journey as your backyard garden evolves.

Swimming Pools

Once considered a luxury, swimming pools are becoming a common landscape feature: a wide range of styles and prices makes it easier than ever to add a pool to your home.

When thinking about what sort of pool to install, start by deciding how you plan to use it, and then select the features you'll need. If diving is your passion, you'll want depth. A lap pool, in contrast, can be shallow (only 4 to 5 feet deep) and narrow, but it will require considerable length. Usage by small children

dictates a wide, shallow area for nonswimmers (for more on pool safety, see page 74). A pool just for cooling off or floating a raft or two can be much smaller than one that routinely accommodates groups of rambunctious teens. If cost or space is an issue, consider an aboveground pool: it's less of an investment than the in-ground sort, is often easier to install on a sloping site, and, when landscaped with decking and plantings, can be as attractive as an in-ground structure.

Pools typically come in rectangular, oval, L, square, kidney, angular, free-form, and round shapes. Depending on the pool's construction, it's also possible to create your own design, though this will typically increase the price. Match the shape of the pool to your house and garden. If you have a Colonial home with formal plantings, for instance, a rectangular or L-shaped pool will fit in better than a curvilinear one.

A pool does tend to dominate the landscape year-round, but that doesn't mean you can't integrate it into the surroundings if you want it to blend in more. Depending on the garden's overall style, you might use native stone paving, a dark liner or dark-colored plaster that gives the water the look of a lagoon, a softly curving shape, a built-in stream or waterfall, or planting pockets at the water's edge. All of these features will give a more natural look.

Another factor to consider when adding a pool is the paved area or deck that will surround the water. If you'll be entertaining often, try to incorporate a space that's at least equal to the area of the pool itself. Not only will this give you plenty of room for guests, tables, and chairs, it will help isolate lawns and flower beds from the pool; otherwise, swimmers will inevitably drag plant debris and soil into the water.

The most common repair for older pools is replastering, which fixes minor cracks, hides stains, or changes the pool's color. You can also install new trim tile or replace the coping to dramatically improve the look of an outdated pool.

TOP *Arching sprays from decorative fountains add the soothing sound of falling water to this graceful pool. Underwater lights lend drama after dark.*

ABOVE *The natural look of this pool is enhanced by overhanging stones and plantings.*

Pools and Regulations

Before building a swimming pool, check into the legal requirements set forth in deed restrictions, zoning laws, and building, health, and safety codes. Also familiarize yourself with the building codes that apply to related structures, such as decks and fences.

In-ground pools are constructed either from sprayed concrete on a steel-reinforced frame or from thick vinyl suspended on a sturdy frame. Concrete pools offer the advantages of durability and design flexibility; in addition, you can choose an interior finish of paint, plaster, or tile (in ascending order of cost). With a vinyl pool, shape is limited to what the manufacturer offers, and your choice of interior finish boils down to the color of the liner. The advantages of vinyl pools are that they're less expensive than concrete and more quickly installed. They are also less durable, but you can still expect a high-quality vinyl liner to last at least 10 years; any tears can usually be repaired without draining the water.

Tucked into a landscape of predominantly native plants, a spa spills over a stone weir to the pool below. Positioned close to an outdoor fireplace, the spa extends the bathing season through most of the year.

Pool Safety

For pool owners with young children or grandchildren (or young visitors or neighbors), water accidents are a constant threat. That's why all swimming pools must have a fence or other barrier to limit access.

Though height requirements vary, most communities require that properties with pools have a fence that encloses the pool area completely. The fence should have self-closing gates with self-latching mechanisms beyond the reach of young children. Any vertical bars should be no more than 4 inches apart; there should be no crossbars or other horizontal members that could provide toeholds for climbing. The area outside the fence should be kept clear of chairs or other objects that a child could use to boost himself over. If the pool is aboveground, you must be able to remove or block the ladder or steps that lead up to it.

If your entire yard is already fenced, you may have to add a second fence around the pool, but check with your building inspector to make certain. Most municipalities specify a minimum distance from water's edge to yard fence, and the yard fencing must also fulfill safety requirements.

Doors and windows that lead directly from house to pool can be made more secure with additional locks installed at least 5 feet high. For sliding glass doors, options include locks for the top of the moving panel and its frame, automatic sliding-door closers that prevent the door from standing open, and removable bars that mount to the frame.

Another factor to consider is the decking material surrounding the pool. Most pool-related accidents involve slips and falls, so the decking must have a slip-resistant, textured surface. It also must drain properly, to avoid puddles of standing water.

Keeping Cool

During a Southern summer, you can count on heat and humidity hammering away for months on end. That hot, relentless sun can make outdoor activities about as inviting as spending the day in a steam room—but fortunately, there are ways to fight back. A swimming pool can help, of course (see pages 72–73); taking a dip is a great way to cool off at any hour. But water can bring relief in other forms, too. Try installing spray misters in a gazebo roof, for example; especially when combined with fans, the fine spray can create a welcome oasis of cooling breezes.

Out in the garden, think about creating shade at the south and west sides of the house, where hot afternoon sun strikes hardest. Plant shade trees in these hot spots, providing you don't mind waiting a few years for them to grow. For large areas, choose tall, relatively fast-growing trees with ascending branches, such as Japanese zelkova, Chinese pistache, tulip poplar, and red maple. For smaller areas such as patios, choose shorter, less messy trees (see page 137).

Sometimes you just can't wait for relief. In that case, consider building an arbor over a seating area; the rafters will cast broken shade right away. Increase the shade by training vines up the structure. An awning or umbrella provides instant shelter from the sun.

You feel more comfortable in a warm, sticky room when there's a fan blowing on you. The same principle applies outdoors. Determine the direction of prevailing summer breezes, then orient your garden or sitting area to take advantage of them.

Solid fences, walls, and hedges block air movement. But lattice fences and openwork brick walls allow breezes to pass through. You can also increase air movement by building an elevated deck instead of one at ground level, and installing one or more sturdy fans in arbors and gazebos.

During summer hot spells, temperatures downtown often exceed those in the countryside by 5 or 6 degrees—all of that asphalt and concrete in the city radiates heat. The same is true in your garden. The more paving or bare soil it contains, the hotter it will be. The more lawn, ground cover, and planting beds it has, the cooler it will be. Light-colored paving doesn't feel as hot underfoot, but it often produces uncomfortable glare. One solution—tint concrete gray or choose gray or tan-colored gravel and stone.

Small Garden Spaces

Not every garden has sweeping vistas and towering trees. Some Southerners work with only an intimate courtyard or small patio—or perhaps a balcony with just enough room for a comfy chair and a few scented geraniums. And even if you have a good-sized garden, it's often the small spaces (a little path lined with pots, a shady nook by the entry) that become favorite spots for outdoor relaxation. In close quarters, every detail is important (for an excellent example, see pages 30–31), so you may find yourself paying more attention to making everything harmonize just so—and in turn, getting more out of your gardening experience.

If you do want to make the space seem larger, here are a few tried-and-true techniques. First, think vertically: use vines clambering up a wall or weaving through a trellis, hanging baskets overflowing with blooms, or shelves holding a collection of potted plants at eye level. Second, place a focal point, such as a sculpture or a dramatic specimen plant, as far from the entrance as possible; then make the journey toward the goal an interesting one, perhaps with a zigzag path. Third, divide the area into a series of smaller "rooms" by using horizontal screens or adding a raised or lowered area to create the illusion of a different zone. Just remember: You can think big in even the smallest garden.

FACING PAGE, TOP *Placing a large focal point like this modern water sculpture in a small space adds instant drama.*

BOTTOM FAR LEFT *Stylish and symmetrical, this tiny brick-edged bed takes maximum advantage of available space with a low hedge of boxwood and a carefully trimmed creeping fig.*

BOTTOM LEFT *An arbor dripping with wisteria blooms makes the most of vertical space. See-through furniture gives utility without blocking much visual space.*

TOP RIGHT *In this patio enclave, attention to details—such as the painted floor, a sparkling lighting fixture, and a tinkling wind chime hung on the gate—makes every inch count.*

BOTTOM RIGHT *A small rooftop courtyard is transformed into an elegant garden featuring topiary shrubs and decorative patio furniture.*

Getting Started

How do you turn a bare dirt lot or an overgrown weed patch into an inviting garden? If you haven't tackled such a job before, you may not even know where to begin. But don't worry—step by step, you *can* create the garden you want. This checklist will help you come up with an approach to the project.

❑ Determine your climate zone (see pages 216–217). You'll save time, money, and frustration by choosing plants that are proven performers in your area.

❑ Get to know your soil. To find out whether it is predominantly sand, clay, or loam, do this simple test. Thoroughly wet a small patch of soil; wait for a day, then squeeze a handful firmly in your fist. If it forms a tight ball with a slippery feel, you have clay. If it feels gritty and crumbles apart when you open your hand, it's sandy. A moist yet slightly crumbly ball is closer to loam. To test the soil's pH (acidity or alkalinity), use one of the test kits sold at nurseries. If you'd like a more precise picture of your soil, you can have it tested by a commercial soil laboratory; contact your local Cooperative Extension Office for advice.

❑ Take note of exposure. Is your site open to the sun all day, or is it largely in the shade? Which areas are sunny in the morning but shady in the afternoon (and vice versa)? Will the house, trees, or other large structures cast shade in winter, when the sun is lower in the southern sky, but not in summer, when it arcs more directly overhead?

❑ Make a note of any special conditions that might affect your garden space. For instance, if you're planting where deer frequently browse, you'll need to include a deer fence in your plan or assemble lists of plants that deer are less likely to eat. If your garden is on a steep slope, mowing a lawn would be difficult (and could be unsafe), so you might plant shrubs and ground covers or plan for terraces to mitigate the abrupt grade.

❑ Think about the general style you'd like for your garden. Casual or formal? Tropical or Colonial? Traditional or avant-garde? Now consider the architecture of your home and surroundings, and make sure the style you want will be (or can be modified to be) a good fit.

❑ Jot down a few ideas about how you'd like to use the space. Do you dream of an entertainment area or a private sanctuary—or both? Do you want to grow vegetables and herbs for the table or compose a pretty picture of colorful flowers and foliage— or both? Will children and pets be playing in the garden?

❑ Check local zoning and other laws if you plan to do any major construction, and contact your water and utility companies with any questions about underground cabling or water use.

❑ Consider how you can recycle materials like old flagstones or even broken concrete. If you discover large stones when you begin digging a flower bed, think about using them to border a path or even build a small rock garden. If you're tearing down an old fence, you might use the boards to build a compost bin.

❑ Draw a site plan (see pages 56–57). Start by measuring the property's outer boundaries and make a rough sketch as you go. Include all the features of the garden, and indicate the location of your home's doors and windows. Find true north (use a compass) and indicate it on the plan.

❑ Using these measurements, draw a base plan to scale so that you can play around with different possibilities. You can lay a piece of tracing paper over your base plan and see where, for instance, you'd like to locate a pool or rose beds or a bench for enjoying the view.

❑ To get a sense of how your design will look in reality, mock it up by laying out a hose where a curved flower bed might be, or using wooden stakes and string for a hedge's outline. Another option is to use powdered limestone or gypsum (or even flour) to "sketch" free-form shapes on the ground. Bamboo poles—or a person standing with arms held high—can represent tall elements and even help you see how shadows will fall. Use a beach chair to test out different locations for a garden bench, and find out how it feels to sit there in the morning as well as in the afternoon.

❑ Follow basic design principles. Include focal points like a special tree or a piece of art at the end of a sight line. Strive for some degree of symmetry and balance, even with something as simple as a matching pair of plants at the head of a path. Keep proportion in mind; don't try to fill a large space with dozens of tiny annuals when a single sizable shrub suits the spot more comfortably. To achieve a sense of unity and rhythm, repeat a few favorite plants through the garden, and punctuate your composition with accents. Start with a simple design, then embellish it as your garden evolves.

❑ Choose the surfaces for your garden's "floor." If you want a lawn, check with a local nursery for advice on the turf grasses that do well in your area. Would you like to cover a particular patch of ground with a few decorative boulders, or would a fragrant ground cover or a bed of perennials suit you better? If you're putting in paths, decide whether to lay them out with stepping-stones, bricks, gravel, or mulch. Would a flagstone or brick patio meet your needs, or do you prefer a wooden deck? Should your pool be surrounded with plain concrete or decorative pavers?

❑ Next, think about enclosing the space with vertical and overhead elements. A fence may be the quickest and most obvious way to gain privacy, but a hedge or even a small tree can do the job in a softer, more organic way. To shade a dining area, a simple umbrella might suffice, but perhaps you'd prefer an arbor draped with flowering vines.

❑ Remove any dead or unwanted plants from the garden. If you have diseased trees, consult an arborist about whether they can be saved. Some sick-looking plants may actually recover if moved to a more suitable spot; ferns that look burned and parched, for instance, might revive and flourish in a shadier, moister area. And don't be in a hurry to dig up beds before you know exactly what's there; a lovely collection of bulbs just might pop up where you thought nothing was planted. A bland-looking shrub might bloom beautifully in spring or flaunt colorful berries in fall.

❑ Finish any construction and other large-scale projects such as setting boulders or changing grade before you start planting. It's also a good idea to install irrigation systems (see pages 60–61) and lighting before the plants go in. Plant trees and shrubs first, then fill in with vines, perennials, bulbs, and annuals.

CHAPTER 3

Garden Structures

The only limit to
your garden is at the
boundaries of your
imagination.

—*Thomas Church*

Projects with Wood

Lumber of one sort or another is an important component of many landscaping projects. In the following pages, you'll find an overview of the lumber products typically used for garden structures, along with information on various fasteners. You'll also find step-by-step directions for building a board fence (pages 88–89), an arbor (pages 92–93), and a deck (pages 98–99), as well as ideas for creating other structures made of wood.

Selecting Lumber

Because wood comes in so many sizes, species, and grades, a visit to a lumberyard can be a bit overwhelming. To make things easier, write up a detailed list of everything you'll need for your project before you go. You might also take along a plan or sketch of the project. And don't be afraid to ask for help.

SOFTWOOD AND HARDWOOD. Depending on the origin of the wood, lumber is categorized as either *softwood* or *hardwood*. Softwoods come from conifers (such as pine and cypress), while many hardwoods come from deciduous trees. In general, softwoods are much less expensive, easier to work, and more readily available than hardwoods. With the exception of some farmed tropical hardwoods, nearly all outdoor construction is done with softwoods.

SPECIES. Certain kinds of wood—including cypress, cedar, and the tropical hardwood called ipé or ironwood—are naturally resistant to decay. This characteristic, combined with their beauty, makes them ideal for many outdoor projects. However, these woods are too costly to be practical choices for structural members or elements that will be painted or stained. For those parts of an outdoor structure, substitute other, less expensive types of softwoods, or use pressure-treated lumber

Build a Fence

Construct an Arbor

Build a Deck

(see facing page). For information on plastic and composite lumber, see page 85.

LUMBER GRADES. At the lumber mill, wood is sorted and graded according to several factors: natural growth characteristics (such as knots), defects (see facing page), and commercial drying and preserving techniques that affect its strength, durability, and appearance. A stamp on each piece of lumber tells you its moisture content, grade, and species, as well as the mill that produced it and the grading agency (often SPIB, Southern Pine Inspection Bureau).

As a rule, the higher the grade, the more expensive the lumber. Bear in mind, though, that the highest grade isn't always the best choice for every element of a structure. Do your research and find out just which grade of lumber is right for each part of your project.

Structural lumber and timbers (see "Lumber Sizes," facing page) are graded for strength. The most common grading system includes the grades Select Structural, No. 1, No. 2, and No. 3. For premium strength, choose Select Structural. Lumberyards often sell a mix of grades called No. 2 and Better. Other grading systems used for some lumber (typically 2 by 4s) classify wood as Construction, Standard, or Utility, or as a mixture of grades called Standard and Better.

Cedar grades you're likely to see, starting with the highest quality, are Architect Clear, Custom Clear, Architect Knotty, and Custom Knotty. These grades don't indicate if wood is heartwood or sapwood, but that distinction does affect price. *Heartwood*, the darker, denser part of the wood from the tree's core, is more resistant to rot, so it's also pricier. *Sapwood*—the lighter, less dense wood from the outer part of the trunk—is less durable, but it's also less expensive.

DEFECTS. Lumber is subject to a number of defects due to weathering and milling errors. To check, lift each piece and look down the face and edges; the lumber should be straight, not warped or curved. Also be on the lookout for rotting, staining, splits, and *wane*—missing wood or untrimmed bark along the edges or corners of the piece. Look for insect holes and reservoirs of sap (pitch), as well.

LUMBER SIZES. Lumber is divided into categories according to size: *dimension lumber*, which ranges from 2 to 4 inches thick and is at least 2 inches wide; *timbers*, heavy structural lumber at least 5 inches thick; and *boards*, which are normally not more than 1 inch thick and 4 to 12 inches wide.

When you shop, remember that a so-called 2 by 4 does not actually measure 2 inches by 4 inches. The designation "2 by 4" is its *nominal size*, referring to its measurements before drying and surface-planing. The finished size is actually 1½ by 3½ inches. Likewise, a nominal 4 by 4 is really 3½ by 3½ inches.

Rough lumber is usually closer to the nominal size, because it is wetter and has not been surface-planed. When measurements are critical, be sure to check the actual dimensions of any lumber before you buy.

Finishing Wood

Structural elements that contact soil or are embedded in concrete do not require a finish. But to protect the aboveground parts of a structure and preserve their beauty, you'll want to apply a water repellent or a stain. Whatever product you choose, try it on a sample board first. And always read labels: some products should not be applied over new wood, and others may require a sealer first.

Pressure-treated Lumber

Wood that has been pressure treated with certain preservatives can survive outdoors for decades longer than untreated lumber. For many years, the most widely available product was lumber containing chromated copper arsenate (CCA), but this has now been phased out for residential use due to concerns about its arsenic content. Replacements include pressure-treated lumber containing copper and the fungicide azole, often sold as CA-B, and ACQ (alkaline copper quaternary treated lumber). You can buy these pressure-treated lumbers manufactured for use either

These steps are fronted with heavy, pressure-treated timbers.

aboveground (for decks and fence rails, for example) or in-ground (as for posts). Check the tag stapled to the end of each piece to be sure you are buying lumber appropriate to your needs. Some of the newer aboveground types are smooth rather than perforated, making them more attractive.

When building with pressure-treated lumber, don't use aluminum hardware and flashing: it tends to corrode quickly when in contact with chemically treated wood. Instead, use hot-dipped galvanized or stainless steel fasteners (or check with your supplier for other recommendations). Cutting the lumber to size will expose untreated wood, so brush the cut ends with a preservative, following manufacturer's directions.

All pressure-treated lumber contains chemicals, so observe precautions when you work with it. Wear safety glasses and a dust mask when cutting; always wear gloves, and wash your hands thoroughly when you've finished working. Be sure to launder your work clothes separately. Dispose of scraps and sawdust by ordinary trash collection; don't use them for mulch or compost. Never burn treated wood in open fires, fireplaces, or stoves.

Because certain chemicals may migrate into soil, some manufacturers also suggest lining raised planting beds constructed of treated lumber with an impervious liner, such as heavy polyethylene.

Fasteners and Hardware

Nails, screws, bolts, and metal framing connectors are all essential elements of wooden garden structures. The hardware you'll typically need for various projects is described here.

Nails

For outdoor construction, use hot-dipped galvanized, aluminum, or stainless steel nails; these types resist rust. (*Note:* When using pressure-treated lumber, *do not* use aluminum fasteners or hardware; the preservatives in the lumber cause aluminum to corrode quickly.) You can use either common or box nails; the two are similar to each other, but common nails have a thicker shank. This makes them more difficult to drive, but increases their holding power. Both types are sold in boxes or loose in bins. Standard nail sizes are given by the "penny" (abbreviated "d"); the higher the penny number, the longer the nail. Equivalents in inches for the most widely used nails are as follows: 4d = 1½ inches; 6d = 2 inches; 8d = 2½ inches; 10d = 3 inches; 16d = 3½ inches; 20d = 4 inches.

Choose nails that have a length about twice the thickness of the material through which you will be nailing. Most decking, fencing, and overhead framing should be secured with 6d, 8d, or 16d nails.

Deck Screws

Although they're more expensive than nails, galvanized deck screws have several advantages. They don't pop up as readily, their coating is less likely to be damaged during installation, and using them eliminates hammer dents in your decking. What's more, they are surprisingly easy to drive into softwoods such as cypress and cedar, especially if you use an electric drill or screw gun. Screws are not rated for

shear (hanging) strength, so use nails, bolts, or lag screws (also called lag bolts), to fasten heavy members such as joists or beams to cross members. The heavy-duty *lag screw* has a square or hexagonal head that you tighten with a wrench or a ratchet and socket.

For decks, choose screws that are long enough to penetrate joists at least as deep as the decking is thick (for 2-by-4 or 2-by-6 decking, buy 3-inch screws).

Bolts

For heavy-duty fastening, choose bolts. Most are zinc-plated steel, but aluminum and brass are also available. Bolts go in predrilled holes that are secured by nuts. The *machine bolt* has a square or hexagonal head that must be tightened with a wrench; the *carriage bolt* has a self-anchoring head that digs into the wood as the nut is tightened. *Expanding anchor bolts* allow you to secure wooden members to a masonry wall.

Bolts are classified by diameter (⅛ to 1 inch) and length (⅜ inch and up). To give the nut a firm bite, select a bolt ½ to 1 inch longer than the combined thicknesses of the pieces to be joined.

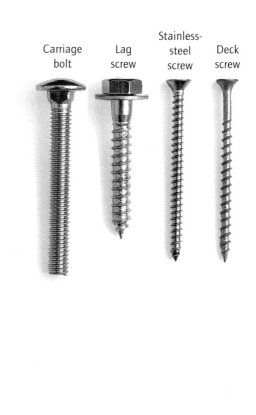

Ring shank nail

Common nail

Finishing nail

Carriage bolt

Lag screw

Stainless-steel screw

Deck screw

Framing Connectors

The photos show several framing connectors. Galvanized metal connectors can help prevent lumber splits caused by toenailing two boards together. Be sure to attach connectors with the fasteners specified by the manufacturer.

To eliminate visible fasteners, *deck clips* can be nailed to the sides of decking lumber and secured to joists. In addition to remaining hidden between the deck boards, they elevate the boards slightly off the joists, discouraging the rot that wood-to-wood contact may cause. However, clips are more expensive and more time-consuming to install than nails or screws.

Framing connectors and hardware, clockwise from top right: post anchors, deck post tie, strengthening straps, rigid tie corner, joist hangers, rigid flat tie, and decorative post tops.

Plastic and Composite Building Materials

"Lumber" made from recycled plastic is rapidly gaining popularity for building decks and other landscaping structures. This long-lasting product requires almost no maintenance beyond periodic cleaning, and it comes pre-finished, though some kinds can be stained or painted (check with the manufacturer for suitable finish materials). Most plastic lumber can be cut, drilled, and installed just like solid wood, but it won't splinter or crack like wood does. And as an additional advantage, it diverts plastic from landfills. Some types are intended solely for decking, but others can also be used for deck rails, stair treads and risers, edgings, and raised-bed borders.

Composite lumber is made of recycled plastic mixed with sawdust or other natural material that gives the planks a more woodlike look. The boards you buy may be solid, hollow-core, or tongue-and-groove in design. The strength of composite lumber for decking varies from product to product, but most cannot span the same distance as an equal amount of solid wood. Follow the manufacturer's instructions for design and installation.

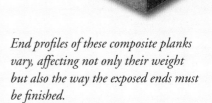

End profiles of these composite planks vary, affecting not only their weight but also the way the exposed ends must be finished.

Fences and Gates

Fences and outdoor screens can transform a garden into a secure, attractive retreat from the outside world. When well designed, they filter the sun's glare, turn a brisk wind into a pleasant breeze, and reduce noise levels. Fences and screens also make effective partitions, dividing the yard into separate areas for recreation, relaxation, vegetable gardening, and storage. Fences serve many of the same purposes as walls (see page 122), but they're generally less formal in appearance, easier to construct, and less expensive.

Wooden balustrades mimic stone for a timeless look. This fence is well suited to the aged brick pathway.

Choosing a Fence

Begin by choosing the size and style of the fence according to its function. For example, a tall board fence may be the best option for a privacy screen, but a more open design will work better as an edging for the vegetable garden. (Most communities have regulations restricting fence height; check with your local building department. If desired, you can add more height by training vines to twine along the top of the fence.) Then double-check that the style and materials you've chosen coordinate with your house, landscaping, and other established or planned garden structures.

A CLASSIC GATE

Latch secures gate to post

Most fences are built partly or entirely of wood. These commonly come in three basic types: post-and-rail, picket, and solid board. You can include louvers, slats, lattices, or trellises if you want to frame or "edit" views. Alternatives to wood include vinyl, galvanized wire, plastic mesh, and ornamental iron. Vinyl fences are readily available, easy to maintain, and quite simple to install.

If your fence will be on or near a boundary line, make certain you have the property line clearly established (see "Digging In," pages 50–79). To minimize potential conflicts with your neighbors, it's wise to have a written agreement concerning fence design and location. An easy way to keep everyone happy is to build a fence that looks equally good on both sides.

Choosing a Gate

Gates can offer access to your garden, frame a view, or—along with the fence—make a definite design statement. You may decide to build a gate that closely matches the fence in style and materials, but you can also opt for contrast—such as a metal gate set into posts of a wooden fence. A low picket gate or one of airy lath invites visitors in with its open, friendly appearance; a high, solid gate may be less inviting, but it provides more security and privacy for those within.

The minimum width for a gate is usually 3 feet, but an extra foot creates a more gracious, welcoming feel. If you anticipate moving gardening or other equipment through the gate, make the opening even wider. For an extra-wide space, consider a two-part gate or even a gate on rollers designed for a driveway.

A basic gate consists of a rectangular frame with a diagonal brace running from the bottom corner of the hinge side of the gate to the top corner of the latch side. Use pressure-treated or other rot-resistant wood. Siding fastened to the frame completes the gate.

Choose strong galvanized hinges and latches. It's better to select hardware that's heftier than you need than to risk something too flimsy. Attach both hinges and latches with galvanized screws.

Posts may be capped with decorative finials

Hinges must be strong enough to support the gate

Hinge clearance

Frame is built from 2 × 4s; diagonal brace prevents gate from sagging

Footing is poured concrete, typically ⅓ the post depth

Gravel base aids drainage; rock helps keep posts from rotting

Building a Board Fence

In general, fence-building is a straightforward task. The hardest part is sinking the posts; use a posthole digger or power auger to make the job easier. The procedure outlined here is a good one for putting up a basic board fence.

Before you set a post or pound a nail, check your local building and zoning codes, as they may influence style, materials, setback, and other requirements. Then tackle the building stages: plotting the fence, installing posts, and finally adding rails and siding.

For fences from 3 to 6 feet tall, plan to set posts at least 2 feet deep—12 inches deeper for end and gate posts. For taller fences, the rule of thumb for post depth is one-third the post length. You can either dig

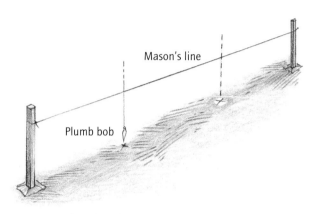

1. First, mark each end or corner post location with a stake. Run mason's line between the stakes, as shown. With chalk, mark remaining post locations on the line. Using a level or plumb bob, transfer each mark to the ground and drive in additional stakes. Then dig holes 6 inches deeper than post depth, making them 2½ to 3 times the post's diameter.

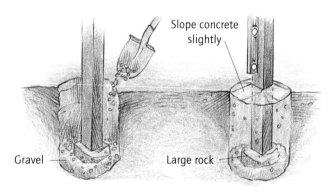

2. Place a large, flat rock at the base of each hole and add 4 to 6 inches of gravel. Place post in hole and shovel in concrete, tamping it down with a broomstick or capped steel pipe. Adjust the post for plumb with a level. Continue filling until the concrete extends 1 or 2 inches above ground level, and slope it away from the post to divert water.

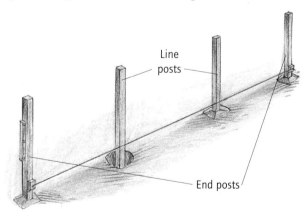

3. To align posts, first position the 2 end or corner posts so their faces are parallel, then plumb them and set them permanently. Use spacer blocks and a mason's line to locate line posts, spacing each a block's thickness from the line. After setting posts in fresh concrete, you have about 20 minutes to align them before concrete hardens. Let cure for 2 days.

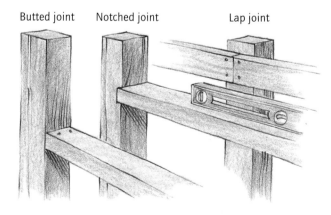

4. Brush on wood preservative where rails and posts will meet. Then fasten one end of each rail; check level with a helper and secure the other end. You can butt them against the post and toenail them, notch them in (cut notches before installing posts), or lap them over the sides or top of each post. If making lap joints, plan to span at least 3 posts for strength.

postholes to a uniform depth or cut the posts once they are in the ground. Once the posts are installed, the rest of the job is easy, especially when you have one or two helpers.

If you're planning to hang a gate, too, see pages 86–87 for pointers on construction and design.

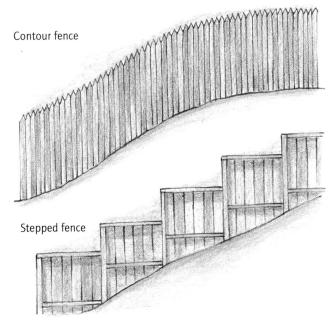

Contour fence

Stepped fence

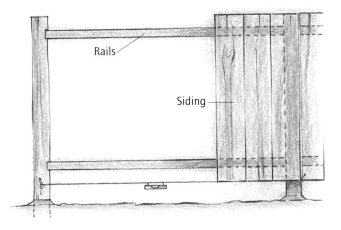

Rails

Siding

5. Cut siding boards to the same length. Stretch and level a line from post to post to mark the bottom of the siding. Check the first board for plumb, then secure it to rails with galvanized nails 3 times as long as the board's thickness. Add additional boards, checking alignment as you go.

6. On a hillside, post-and-rail and solid fences with pickets or grape stakes make good contour fences. Board, louver, basketweave, and panel styles work better for stepped fences, which are more difficult to build. For both kinds, make sure that the bottoms of boards 6 inches or wider are cut to follow the contour of the hillside; otherwise, gaps will remain.

Digging Postholes

Although you can use a pick and shovel to dig postholes for fences (or decks and overheads), some heavier equipment will save you time and effort. Two handy tools are shown here.

Posthole, or clamshell, diggers (near right) work in hard or rocky soil. Spread the handles to open and close the blades, which trap soil. This tool is difficult to use for holes more than 3 feet deep, as the sides of the hole interfere with the spreading of the handles.

A power auger, also known as a power digger or earth drill, is recommended whenever you have more than a dozen holes to dig. You can rent models for operation by one or two people (a two-person model is shown near left), and they may be freestanding or vehicle-mounted. Every so often, pull the auger out of the hole to remove the dirt; a posthole digger or a small spade may also be required.

When you turn the handle of a hand-operated auger, the pointed blades bore into the soil, scraping it up and collecting it in a chamber. Once the chamber is full, remove the auger from the hole and empty out the soil. This tool works best in loose soil.

Arbors and Gazebos

There's nothing quite like an arbor or gazebo to enhance your enjoyment of the garden. These structures furnish shade during the day and shelter during cool evenings, yet are always open to breezes and the enticing scent of flowers. Both give you a place to sit and relax, host a party, or simply mingle with family and friends. They play other, more practical roles as well: they can link house to yard, define different areas of the garden, create a focal point, provide a destination at the end of a path, mask an unattractive feature, or frame a view.

Arbors frame the walls and ceiling of an outdoor room and can be embellished with fragrant or colorful vines (see pages 156–157). You can build arbors in almost any style, from simple archways and airy tunnels to elaborate neoclassical pavilions. By contrast, gazebos lend a feeling of enclosure to those sitting inside, thanks to the solid roof overhead. You'll see them in a number of styles, from old-fashioned Victorian designs to contemporary or rustic motifs.

Arbors work beautifully if located just outside the back (or front) door, where they provide a graceful transition from indoors to out. However, building an arbor or gazebo away from the house can be just as successful. To find the best site, walk around your property, glancing back at the house. Look for a vantage point that provides views across the garden (see pages 46–49) and avoids unsightly areas. Consider which exposure you want; if your main deck or patio is in full sun, you may prefer a shady corner, for example. (See "Digging In," pages 50–79.) Then think about the design of the structure itself.

FACING PAGE *An arbor covered with crossvine shades a limestone terrace. Compacted decomposed granite gives the adjacent courtyard a natural look. Both areas offer ample seating for guests.*

ABOVE *A red cedar arbor in a simple design shades a terrace made of Pennsylvania blue-green stone.*

ABOVE RIGHT *Built in the classic style, this airy gazebo offers shade, shelter, and enticing vistas of the surrounding garden. The painted concrete floor echoes the green of lawn and trees.*

RIGHT *Gracefully draped with wisteria, a painted cedar arbor frames a view of the garden and the house beyond.*

Building an Arbor

Building a basic arbor is similar to building other wood garden structures, but you'll probably spend a lot more time on a ladder. These illustrations outline the sequence for erecting a freestanding arbor; for construction details on a house-attached arbor, see the facing page.

Most arbors employ the same basic components (posts, beams, rafters or joists, and roofing), but assembly techniques can vary. Any arbor must conform to spans determined by local building codes—so be sure to check codes before you start to build.

If your arbor will span an existing patio, you can set the posts on footings and piers located outside the

1. Precut posts to length (or run a level line and cut them later). Set posts in anchors embedded in concrete footing or atop precast piers. Hold each post vertical and nail anchor to it.

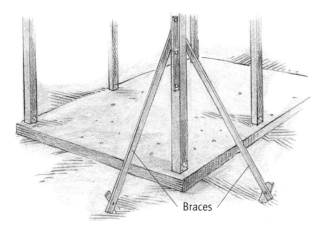

Braces

2. Continue to put up posts, plumbing each post with level on 2 adjacent sides. Secure each in position with temporary braces nailed to wooden stakes that are driven into ground.

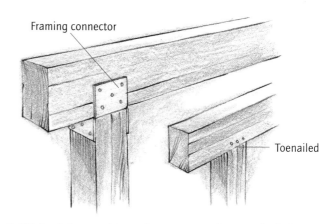

Framing connector

Toenailed

3. With a helper, position a beam on top of posts. Check that posts are vertical and beam is level (adjust, if necessary, with shims); then secure beam to posts.

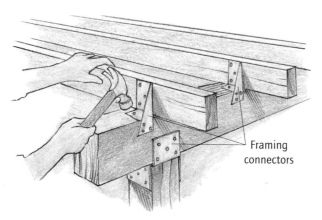

Framing connectors

4. Set and space rafters on top of beams and secure them with framing connectors (shown) or by toenailing to beams. For extra strength, install bracing between beams and posts.

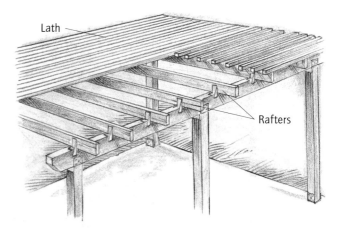

Lath

Rafters

5. Cover rafters with lath, either 1 × 2s or 2 × 2s. Space the lath for plant support or to achieve a specific amount of shade (see facing page).

edge of the patio, or break through the existing paving, dig holes, and pour new concrete footings (and, if necessary, add piers). If you're planning to install a new concrete patio, then you can pour footings and paving at the same time, embedding the post anchors in the wet concrete.

To attach an arbor to your house, you will need to install a ledger, much like a deck ledger (see page 98). Usually made from a 2 by 4 or a 2 by 6, the ledger is typically attached with lag screws—either to wall studs, to second-story floor framing, or to the roof. If the house wall is brick or stone, however, you'll need to drill holes and install expanding anchors to bolt the ledger in place.

Rafters can be set on top of the ledger or hung from it with anchors, joist hangers, or rafter hangers. If your arbor's roof will be flat, simply square up rafter ends. Sloped rafters, however, require angled cuts at each end, plus a notch (as shown at right) where rafters cross the beam.

You can also opt for a solid roofing material such as shingles, siding, or even asphalt. If you leave the structure uncovered, treating it with a preservative or other finish can add years to its life.

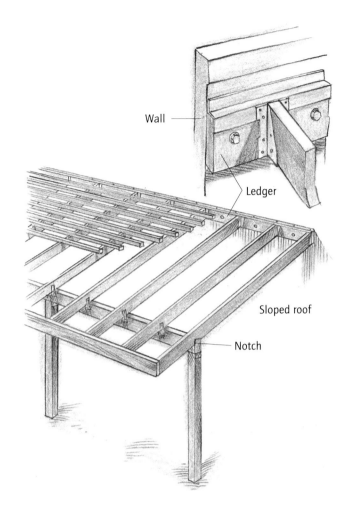

Wall

Ledger

Sloped roof

Notch

Designing for Shade

How shady your arbor is depends in large part on how you arrange the rafters or lath on top. For example, running the rafters east-west provides midday shade. But if you plan on enjoying the arbor more in the early mornings and late afternoons, run these top boards north-south.

How you attach the top boards to the arbor also affects shade. If you stand 1 by 2s or 1 by 3s on edge, they will give little shade at midday when the sun is overhead, but plenty of shade in morning and afternoon when the sun is at an angle. Lay them flat and the result will be exactly the opposite.

On the pitched roof pictured at left, pieces of 2-by-2 lattice, spaced 2 inches apart, were laid atop the rafters. Because they're angled by the pitch of the roof, they create an even greater surface area to block the sun. This arbor provides not only midday shade, but also lots of shade during the afternoon, except for a brief period when the angle of the sun matches the angle of the lattice pieces.

Use these ideas as general guidelines. Which design is better for you depends on where you live, the side of the house the arbor is located on, the shape and size of the arbor, and other factors. You might want to experiment with the placement of a few top boards before attaching them permanently to the structure.

An Easy-to-build Pergola

Constructed with four ready-made wooden arches bought at a nursery, this pergola—a series of arches "roofed" with lath and vines—defines and decorates a narrow side yard. Each wooden arch has a pair of frames spaced 2 feet apart with an opening wide enough to bridge a 4-foot-wide path. After painting the arches, the owners spaced them evenly along the house wall, set the legs in concrete, and nailed the arches to the wall on one side. They linked the tops of the four arches with 2 by 2s, butted end to end. The leaves and delicate pink blossoms of climbing roses spill over the curving tops of the arches, brush against the windows of the house, and dangle into the tunnel-like passage below.

You could also set a series of purchased arbors over a sunny pathway leading to the vegetable garden, and plant a climber to cover it. Or, for a charming focal point, you might opt for a single structure made of an arch and lattice panels to shelter a garden bench.

Purchasing Arbors and Trellises

Many homeowners don't have the time or inclination to build their own garden structures. Fortunately, it's easy to find interesting, good-quality arbors and trellises at nurseries and through mail-order suppliers.

Ready-made arbors range from simple metal arches to more complex wooden structures constructed of rot-resistant lumber. Most are designed to fit over a garden path; a clever way to link several wooden arches is shown above.

Trellises and lattices of various sorts are also widely available. Use them to decorate a blank wall or as freestanding screens; all are delightful covered with twining vines. Trellises fashioned from woven twigs or vines bring a rustic touch to the garden, while the architectural wooden and metal ones generally look more formal. Prefabricated (or custom-made) lattice panels offer further possibilities.

Custom-made lattice panels decorate a garage wall. The panels are mounted on top of 2-by-4 spacers; these enhance the panels' looks by adding depth and shadows, and provide room for vines to climb. A 1-by-4 facing board conceals the junction of two panels. The inset "window" and wall fountain provide a focal point.

Gazebos

There are many designs for gazebos (also called belvederes or summerhouses), but most adhere to the same basic plan. All require a foundation, posts or walls, beams, rafters, and some type of roofing. Cramped quarters are no fun, so make your gazebo at least 8 feet tall, with sufficient floor space (at least 8 by 8 feet) to easily accommodate several pieces of furniture.

Support for a gazebo typically comes from a simple post-and-beam frame built of sturdy rot-resistant or pressure-treated lumber. A gazebo roof may take a variety of forms. The most traditional one—a six- or eight-hub style—is also by far the trickiest to lay out; a roof with four sides is much more straightforward. If the roof is made of solid materials (and most are), remember that it must be pitched to allow water to run off. Framing connections are most easily made by means of readily available prefabricated metal fasteners (see page 85).

Gazebo Kits

If building an entire gazebo from scratch seems overwhelming, look into building one from a kit. Several companies manufacture traditional gazebos in kit form, complete except for the foundation. You construct the gazebo atop a concrete slab, deck, or foundation of piers or crushed stone. For most types, assembly takes only a weekend or two and requires just basic tools and skills and the assistance of a helper.

Though kits do cost less than custom gazebos, they can still be expensive, so be sure you know what you're getting. Connections should be made with galvanized or brass hardware, and machining should be done carefully so that assembly is relatively easy. Find out whether the gazebo is made from rot-resistant lumber such as cedar heartwood or from a less expensive softwood or pressure-treated lumber. Also check into finishes—can the wood be finished naturally, or must it be painted? If the latter, is it available primed for painting?

Finally, make sure you know what's included in the price of the kit. Who pays for delivery? Are the flooring and floor framing included? What about benches, screens, and steps? Many kits allow you to choose between open railings or lattice panels and other finishing details.

Decks

A traditional deck, attached directly to an exterior house wall, serves as an extension of the home's interior, becoming a welcoming outdoor room and offering a space where family members and guests can mingle and circulate between house and garden. Locating a deck away from the house offers different possibilities: a detached deck becomes a destination point, offering a quiet retreat among trees and shrubs. Adding an arbor for enclosure or a water fountain for soothing sound enhances the feeling of a hideaway.

Why build a deck rather than a patio? Your site may be a determining factor. A deck can bridge bumps and slopes or "float" over swampy areas that might sink a brick patio. Decking lumber is resilient underfoot, and because it doesn't store heat the way masonry can, it's cooler than a patio (a real consideration in hot-weather areas). In some cases, a low-level deck is a good replacement for an existing cracked or worn concrete slab— you can often use the slab as a base for the deck.

A low-level deck is the simplest kind to build and is well within the scope of most do-it-yourself home

ABOVE *Built out over a hillside, this deck feels like a tree house. A wooden bench wraps around the mature trees that provide shade; holes cut in its surface accommodate the trunks.*

LEFT *Built at grade level, this inviting deck was designed to take advantage of the surrounding trees' shade—and to preserve their roots.*

BELOW *Composite lumber makes this sunny deck nearly maintenance-free.*

projects. However, decks that are cantilevered out from an upper story or over water or a promontory should be designed by a structural engineer and installed by a professional. Decks on steep hillsides or unstable soil should also receive professional attention. Be sure to check local building codes as you plan any style of deck.

To surface your deck, use rot-resistant lumber, such as refined-looking cedar or cypress heartwood, farmed tropical hardwood, or less expensive pressure-treated lumber (see pages 82–83). Composite lumber (see page 85) is an increasingly popular choice for decking. For the underpinnings—posts, beams, and joists— choose pressure-treated lumber. It's a good idea to review the information on hardware given on pages 84–85 before building a deck.

Overheads, benches, railings, and steps are often integral to a deck's framing. While it may be possible to add these extras later, it's easier to design and build the whole structure at once. While you're planning, think about whether you'll need to install plumbing pipes or electrical wiring for outlets and light fixtures.

Most wooden decks will need periodic treatment with a wood preservative or stain to prevent water absorption and reduce the expansion and contraction that lead to cracking, splintering, and warping.

Build a Deck

Building a Low Deck

While not especially difficult, building a low-level deck attached to the house is a project that goes much more quickly with a helper or two. Plan on a few weekends of work to construct the deck.

Be sure the completed deck will be at least 1 inch below adjacent access doors to keep water and snow outside. If you're planning a freestanding deck, substitute an extra beam and posts for the ledger shown; extra bracing at the corners may also be necessary.

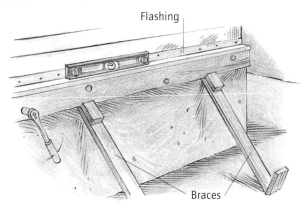

Flashing

Braces

1. Determine the position of the ledger and prop it into place with 2 × 4 blocks or braces. Drill staggered holes for lag screws every 16 inches, then fasten ledger in place, making sure it is level. To prevent rot, either space the ledger off the wall with blocks or washers, or add metal flashing, as shown.

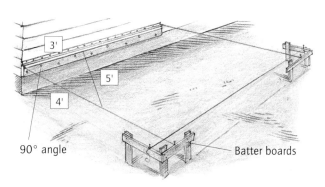

3'

5'

4'

90° angle · Batter boards

2. Batter boards mark height of deck; build them at outside corners, level with the ledger top. To mark deck edges, run mason's line from batter boards to ledger. Corners must be square; determine using the "3-4-5" triangle method shown.

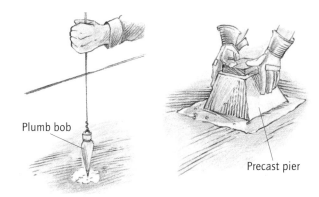

Plumb bob

Precast pier

3. Dangle a plumb bob from mason's lines to mark footings. Dig holes to depths required by code; add gravel, then fill with concrete (see page 88). Push piers into the concrete, level their tops, and let concrete set overnight.

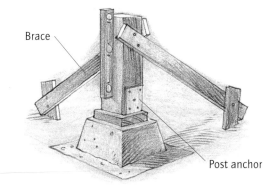

Brace

Post anchor

4. Unless piers have integral post anchors, add them now. Measure and cut posts—for this design, a joist's depth below the top of ledger. Check plumb on 2 sides of each post, temporarily brace each in place, and fasten to piers.

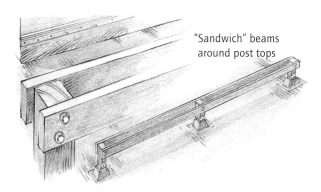

"Sandwich" beams around post tops

5. Position 2-by beams on each side of post tops, as shown. After leveling them with post tops, clamp them in place. Drill staggered holes, then fasten each beam to posts with bolts or lag screws.

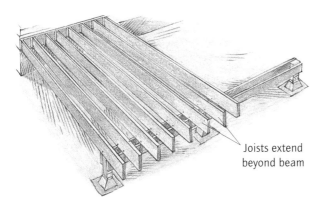

Joists extend
beyond beam

6. *Position joists at predetermined span intervals and secure
to ledger with framing connectors. Set them atop beams and
toenail in place. Brace joists with spacers at open ends and, if
required, at midspan. Add posts for any railings or benches,
or an overhead anchored to deck framing.*

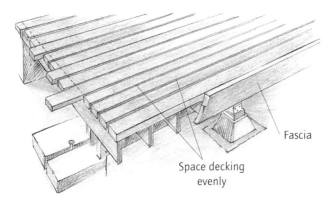

Fascia

Space decking
evenly

7. *Align decking boards atop joists, staggering joints (if any).
Space boards, leaving about ³⁄₁₆ inch—or the thickness of
a 16d nail—for drainage. Fasten decking to joists with 16d
common nails or deck screws. Trim edges with circular saw.*

4 × 4 post

8. *Finish decking ends and edges as desired with fascia boards
or other trim. If you're planning benches, planters, steps, or
railings that aren't tied directly to substructure, add them now.*

ABOVE *This deck light automatically
turns on at dusk, illuminating steps and
other deck surfaces for safety.*

BELOW *Decking patterns don't always have to
involve parallel designs. Here, the bull's-eye pattern
sets off the gazebo and palm trees effectively.*

Child's Play Structure

Play structures are increasingly popular choices for children's backyard play equipment. Most combine traditional swings and slides with a fort or hideout and a place for a sandbox; other fun features, such as a climbing wall or net, are also available.

When planning for a play structure, be sure to allow plenty of space. You'll need at least 6 feet clear of all obstacles around the structure. In addition, the safety zone at the bottom of a slide should equal the height of the slide plus 4 feet; swings need a safety zone two times the height of the swing set. To ensure soft landings, cushion the ground inside the entire safety zone with a 6- to 9-inch-thick layer of wood mulch, wood chips, or sand.

Companies that specialize in manufactured play structures sell kits with all the necessary parts, including lumber already cut to size, drilled for most or all bolts, smoothed, and stained. You can have the kit professionally assembled at your home (for a fee of several hundred dollars) or put it together yourself, using the detailed instructions supplied with the kit. To help you decide, the steps pictured here show how Tony Lerma, a professional installer for Rainbow Play Systems, erected a simple play structure in 2½ hours.

1 *The bottom braces on the fort are attached to the legs with lag screws. Holes for this type of screw are not predrilled—and there are 121 of them in this structure. Lerma drives one in with a ½-inch impact wrench in about 1 second. If you're using a socket wrench, you'll need to predrill every hole and then tighten the screw with the wrench.*

2 *To erect the legs without a helper, Lerma wraps his leg around a post to hold it in an upright position while attaching another bottom brace. When both leg assemblies are up, he pushes mulch under low spots until his level shows that the structure is flat.*

3 *The flooring sections are pre-assembled at the factory, so Lerma only needs to bolt them in place. He tightens the nuts after checking that the diagonal distance between opposite corners is equal; this shows that the floor is square.*

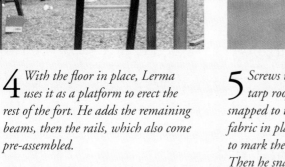

4 *With the floor in place, Lerma uses it as a platform to erect the rest of the fort. He adds the remaining beams, then the rails, which also come pre-assembled.*

5 *Screws with snap heads hold the tarp roof in place. With the screws snapped to the fabric, Lerma drapes the fabric in place and taps with a hammer to mark the locations for the screws. Then he snaps off the screws and fastens them to the wood.*

6 *After attaching the ladder and the slide, Lerma builds the swing beam support structure. With a special A-frame brace loosely bolted to the legs and the swing beam, he rests one beam end on the fort and hoists the other to allow the legs to swing underneath for support.*

Projects with Masonry

The following pages offer an introduction to popular masonry materials for landscaping projects, including stone, artificial rock, brick, pavers, and concrete. You'll also find step-by-step directions to help you lay brick in sand (pages 110–111) and masonry in mortar (pages 112–113). Pages 118–119 walk you through installing a brick-bordered gravel path, and page 123 shows you how to build a dry stone wall.

Shopping for Stone

Stone is particularly appealing for landscaping—it's a natural material, and most types are very durable. Bear in mind, though, that the availability of types, shapes, sizes, and colors varies by locality; and some stone can cost up to five times as much as concrete or brick. Geography plays a big part in price: the farther you live from the quarry, the more you'll have to pay. Some dealers sell stone by the cubic yard, which simplifies ordering; others sell it by the ton. Your supplier can help you calculate how much you'll need.

STONES FOR PAVING. Many stones are precut in square or rectangular shapes; these are fairly uniform in thickness and easy to lay in a grid pattern. Others come in more random widths and thicknesses.

Sandstone and *limestone* are popular paving choices. They're more porous than other types and usually have a chalky or gritty texture. Another excellent selection is *slate*, a fine-grained, dense, smooth rock.

Granite and *marble* are both valued for their hardness and durability. Marble does look beautiful in

Lay Masonry Surfaces

Install a Gravel Path

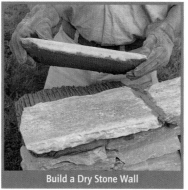
Build a Dry Stone Wall

formal settings, but it's rather expensive for most garden construction. Equally lovely in a formal garden—and not as pricy—are *flagstones* and *cut stone tiles.* Technically, flagstone is any flat stone that is either naturally thin or split from rock that cleaves easily. It blends well with plantings and with ponds and other water features. Furthermore, it's one of the few paving materials that can be set directly on stable soil. However, outdoor furniture and objects with wheels do sometimes catch on its irregular surface, and some types get dirty easily (and may be difficult to clean).

Fieldstone, river rock, and *pebbles* are less expensive than flagstone and cut tiles. These water-worn or glacier-ground stones produce rustic, uneven pavings that make up in charm what they may lack in smoothness underfoot. Smaller stones and pebbles can be set or seeded into concrete to make exposed aggregate paving. Cobblestones can be laid in concrete or on tamped earth; narrow mosaic panels of very small stones can be used as a design element to break up an expanse of concrete or brick.

For economy, good drainage, and a more casual look, don't forget *gravel* and *crushed rock,* both of which can make good paving. Gravel is collected or mined from natural deposits; crushed rock is mechanically fractured and graded to a uniform size. When choosing gravel, consider color, sheen, texture, and size. Take home samples as you would paint chips, and keep in mind that gravel color, like paint color, looks more intense when spread over a large area.

STONES FOR WALLS. There are two broad classes of stone that work well for walls: *rubble* (untrimmed)

and *ashlar* (trimmed). Partially trimmed pieces such as *cobblestones* can also create attractive effects.

The stones used in rubble walls may be rounded from glacial or water action; examples include river rock and fieldstone. These stones are difficult to cut, so it's usually easier to search for rocks of the size you need. Rubblestone is frequently the cheapest stone available for walls.

Ashlar stone is fully trimmed and almost as easy to lay as brick. The flat surfaces and limited range of sizes make formal coursing possible and require less mortar than for rubblework. The most commonly available type of ashlar stone is sandstone; when a tougher stone (such as granite) is cut and trimmed for ashlar masonry, costs are likely to be quite high.

ABOVE *Stones for pavings and walls vary in availability from one region to another, but possible choices include limestone, slate, marble, granite, and a variety of native stone.*

RIGHT *Use loose small stones and gravel alone or with other stones in various sizes to create paths; or seed them into concrete for an exposed aggregate finish.*

Artificial Rock

Rocks and boulders can give the garden an appealingly rugged look. However, big boulders may be hard to find and difficult to transport and set in place; and in some gardens, site conditions can make it difficult to install real stone. For these reasons, many homeowners are turning to artificial rocks (also known as "cultured" stone) that are shaped, textured, and colored to resemble their natural counterparts. Such artificial rocks offer numerous landscaping opportunities. They can form steps and waterfalls; create pockets for plants, lights, or small ponds; or offer concealment for pumps and electrical or water lines. They mask plain retaining walls attractively, as well.

One rock-forming method starts with a boulder-shaped frame of reinforcing bar. Wire mesh or metal lath is secured to the frame; then, several layers of concrete are applied. To mimic the cracks and fissures of natural rock, the still-wet concrete may be carved with tools or embossed with crinkled aluminum foil or other materials.

Another popular technique uses latex models cast on real rocks. The models are sprayed with a mixture of concrete and strands of fiberglass or polypropylene. When the mixture dries, the forms are removed. The result is a thin, sturdy panel with a rock-textured surface. The models yield identical panels, which can be joined together horizontally or vertically.

To imitate the color of true rock—which is generally a pastiche of hues and may also be flecked with lichen—installers color the concrete by brushing, spraying, or spattering on layers of diluted acrylic stains.

These wide, slightly curved steps and low retaining walls are made of artificial cast stone formed directly on the hillside.

Brick

Weather-resistant and durable, brick is a long-time favorite for outdoor projects. And because bricks are small and quite uniform in size, installation is easy.

Two kinds of brick are used for most garden construction: common brick and face brick. Most paving is done with common brick. People like its warm color and texture, and it is less expensive and more widely available than face brick. It's also more porous and less uniform in color and size, with individual bricks varying up to ¼ inch in length.

Face brick, with its sand-finished, glazed surface, is more often used for facing buildings than for garden projects. It does, however, make elegant formal walls and attractive accents, edgings, stair nosings, and raised beds—all outdoor projects where the smooth texture won't present a safety hazard when the brick is wet.

Used brick has uneven surfaces and streaks of old mortar that are attractive in an informal design. Imitation used brick (called "rustic" brick) costs about the same as the genuine article, but it's easier to find and more consistent in quality than most older brick.

Low-density firebrick, blond-colored and porous, is tailor-made for built-in barbecues and outdoor fireplaces. For other uses, it provides interesting accents but doesn't wear as well as common brick.

The standard brick is about 8 by 4 by 2⅜ inches. "Paver" bricks, which are solid and made to use underfoot, are roughly half the thickness of standard bricks. All outdoor bricks are graded according to their ability to withstand weathering. If you live in a region with regular freezes and thaws, choose common bricks rated SX or face bricks rated SW—the rating means they can stand up to severe weather conditions. The staff at a building supply company can help you calculate the quantity of bricks you'll need for your project.

A display of brick includes rough common bricks in various colors, smoother face bricks for accents and edgings, bullnose types (with rounded ends) for stairs and to cap walls, used or imitation used bricks, and precut bricks (such as the triangle, above right) for patterns.

Precast pavers allow you to experiment with designs and shapes, and many imitate tile, brick, or concrete. An assortment is shown here, including stepping-stones, pavers that interlock with puzzlelike shapes, and turf blocks.

Pavers

Easy to install and available in many sizes, colors, and textures, pavers are an ideal material for do-it-yourself masonry projects. Your choices range from simple 12-inch squares to interlocking pavers in a variety of shapes.

Use square pavers to form part of a grid or even a gentle arc. Squares or rectangles can butt together to create broad, unbroken surfaces, or they can be spaced apart and surrounded with grass, a ground cover, or gravel for textural interest.

Interlocking pavers fit together like puzzle pieces. They are made of extremely dense, mechanically pressure-formed concrete. Laid in sand with closed (butted) joints, they create a surface that is more rigid than brick and remains intact even under substantial loads. Some interlocking shapes are proprietary, available at only a few outlets or direct from the distributor. To locate pavers, check the Yellow Pages under Concrete Products.

Modern cobblestone blocks are very popular for casual gardens; butt them tightly together and then sweep sand or soil between the irregular edges. Turf blocks, which have spaces to allow lawn or low ground covers to grow through, are designed to carry light traffic while retaining and protecting the plants. These pavers let you create grassy patios and driveways or side-yard access routes that stand up to wear.

Cast concrete "bricks," available in classic terra-cotta red as well as imitation used or antique styles, have become increasingly popular as substitutes for the real thing because, in many areas, they're significantly less expensive.

Some landscape professionals cast their own pavers in custom shapes, textures, and colors—adobe, stone, and imitation tile, for example. You can also make forms and pour your own pavers, though they won't be as strong as commercial pressure-formed units.

Concrete

Concrete has long been associated with durability, and for good reason. A slab thick enough for its purpose, resting on a bed of firmly tamped gravel, will remain stable for many decades. A properly sized footing provides solid support for a stone or brick wall. And nowadays, concrete is beautiful as well as long-lasting. The variety of molding methods and products makes it possible to create a wide range of textures and colors. And if you eventually get tired of a concrete surface, you can use it as a foundation for a new pavement of stone, brick, or tile set in mortar, as shown on pages 112–113.

Concrete does have a few disadvantages. In some situations, it can seem harsh, hot, glaring, or simply boring. And if smoothly troweled, it can be slick when wet. Moreover, once its dry ingredients are combined with water, you have to work quickly before the mix hardens.

Concrete paving is usually given a surface treatment, both to upgrade its appearance and to improve traction. A heavily or lightly broomed surface is probably the most common. You can also make an exposed aggregate surface, either by uncovering existing aggregate in the concrete mix or seeding small stones in the still-wet concrete. In either case, spray with water and brush away sand and concrete when the surface begins to dry.

Other ways to modify a standard steel-troweled surface include color dusting, staining, acid washing, and finishing with rock salt. To make a stucco-like travertine finish, spatter a stiff concrete-sand mixture over smoothed (but still wet) concrete; after it has partially hardened, scrape the surface with a steel trowel. The resulting texture will be fairly smooth on the high spots, rougher in the low spots. You can also stamp or tint concrete to resemble stone, tile, or brick.

Plan to make the slab for pathways and patios 3 to 4 inches thick; in addition, allow for a 4- to 8-inch layer of compacted gravel below the slab. Forms for concrete are built in the same way as wood edging. For standard paving, you will need 2 by 4s on edge for the forms and 12-inch-long stakes made of 1 by 3s or 1 by 2s to hold the forms in place. If you plan to install dividers in a slab or leave the forms as permanent edging, use rot-resistant or pressure-treated lumber. For curved forms, choose either tempered hardboard, plywood, or, if the forms will be permanent, metal edgings.

To prevent buckling and cracking, reinforce any concrete area more than 8 feet square with 6-inch-

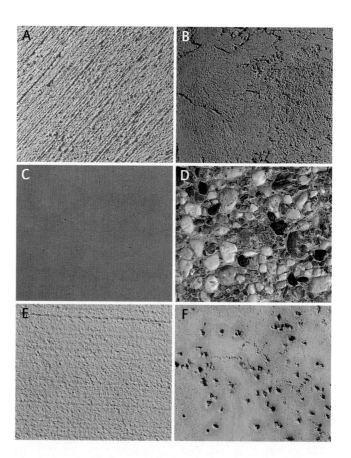

Basic concrete finishes include broomed (A), travertine (B), slick surface (C), exposed aggregate (D), semismooth (E), and rock salt (F).

square welded wire mesh; install it after building the forms. If you're not sure whether your slab needs reinforcement, check with your local building department.

Buying Concrete

Although many people think concrete is just "cement," it's actually a combination of portland cement, sand, aggregate (usually gravel), and water. Portland cement is a complex, finely ground material that undergoes a chemical reaction when mixed with water, becoming a kind of "glue" that binds all the elements of the concrete together. It also gives the finished product its hardness. The sand and aggregate act as fillers and control shrinkage.

Bagged dry, ready-to-use concrete mix is expensive, but it's also convenient, especially for small jobs. A 90-pound bag makes ⅔ cubic feet of concrete, enough to fill one posthole or to cover a 16-inch-square area 4 inches deep.

If your project is fairly large, order the materials in bulk and mix them yourself, either by hand in a heavy-duty wheelbarrow or with a power mixer. Hand mixing is less complicated, but it requires significant exertion. If you have large forms that must be filled in a single pour, it's a good idea to rent a power mixer. Use the following formula for regular concrete (the proportions are by volume): 1 part portland cement, 2¾ parts aggregate, 2½ parts sand, and 1 part water.

Some dealers also supply trailers for wet, ready-mixed concrete that you can haul behind your car. For a larger project (a good-sized patio, for example), plan to have a commercial transit-mix truck deliver enough concrete to finish your project in a single pour. To locate suppliers, look in the Yellow Pages under Concrete, Ready Mixed.

Molding Concrete

To create the look of stones using concrete, you can dig holes or build wooden forms and fill them with concrete. The resulting solid "stepping-stones"—with planting spaces in between—can be textured, smoothed, or seeded with aggregate. Commercial forms like the plastic type shown below are also available; you can use them to make a concrete path resembling a flagstone walkway. Place the form on a clean, level surface (A); use a trowel to fill the mold with concrete (B) and smooth the top. When the concrete is dry enough to hold its shape, remove the mold (C).

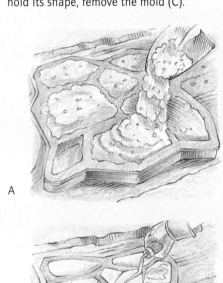

A

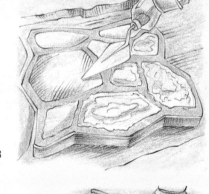

B

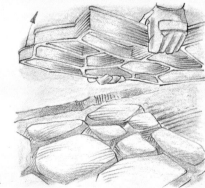

C

Patios and Terraces

Whether you call it a patio or a terrace, a paved outdoor space is a comfortable place for entertaining, dining, or simply relaxing. A terrace is often located just outside the back door, where it serves as a natural transition between indoors and out. However, if space allows, consider a series of patios connected by paths or steps, or a detached patio in a secluded corner of your garden. A neglected side yard might become the site for a private, screened seating area.

There are a number of paving choices for patios and terraces, including masonry units, poured concrete,

and loose materials such as gravel and wood chips. Your choice largely depends on whether you prefer a formal or an informal look. Brick, trimmed stone, and cobblestones look formal if set in mortar in a symmetrical pattern. Irregular flagstones or mossy bricks laid in sand achieve a softer, cottage-garden look, as do spaced concrete pavers.

A smooth poured concrete surface—the first choice for many patios of the past—looks friendlier and less stark if it's finished with seeded aggregate, stamped with a pattern, and/or colored. You can also make

LEFT *An heirloom bronze fountain inspired this lovely formal brick patio. A wide variety of plants brings softness and charm to the setting; a low wall adds a sense of peaceful seclusion.*

ABOVE *Graceful curves give this concrete patio a quiet elegance; naturalistic ground cover plantings help integrate it into the surrounding landscape.*

TOP RIGHT *An island bed filled with perennials helps a small terrace flow into the garden beyond. The mixed flagstone-and-brick paving pattern contributes to the feeling of movement.*

ABOVE RIGHT *A mossy stone patio, reached by mulched paths, blends perfectly with its shady surroundings.*

plain concrete more interesting by including planting pockets in a rectangular concrete slab. Or try pouring the concrete in curved shapes set side by side instead of a single large form; the resulting pads, with planting spaces in between, can be smoothed, colored, and stamped to resemble natural stone.

For economy and a comfortable, casual look, consider loose patio materials such as pea gravel, river rock, or wood chips. These materials blend well with plantings and improve surface drainage as well.

When combined, masonry and low-level wooden decks complement each other and allow flexibility for outdoor areas in shape, texture, and finished height. Although masonry surfaces must rest on solid ground, decks can span sloping, bumpy, or poorly drained areas nearby.

Most patios require an edging of some sort. Repeating the edging material elsewhere (along surface paths, for example) visually links elements in the landscape. Edgings can also connect different areas of a garden: for example, a brick-edged patio might taper off to a brick path that leads to a lawn, also edged with brick.

Laying Brick in Sand

With careful preparation and installation, a brick-in-sand patio or terrace—or even a walk—can prove as durable as bricks set in mortar. And if you decide to change the surface later, you need chip out only one brick to remove the rest intact, regardless of the pattern you choose (see facing page).

Begin by excavating existing soil or sod and spreading 4 to 6 inches of compactible gravel; tamp this firmly in place with a vibrating plate compactor (you can rent one from a masonry supplier or tool rental outlet). Then build permanent edgings around the perimeter to hold both bricks and their bed of sand in place. If you need to cut many bricks, or want to create curved or complex designs, rent a brick saw, also available from a masonry supplier or tool rental outlet (follow the supplier's safety directions carefully).

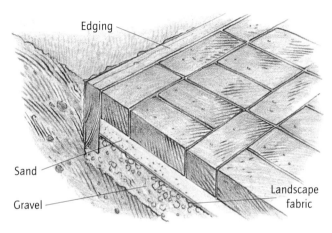

1. This cross section of a typical brick-in-sand patio shows a gravel bed, a layer of landscape fabric to prevent weed growth, packed sand, and wooden edgings. Use rot-resistant lumber for the edgings.

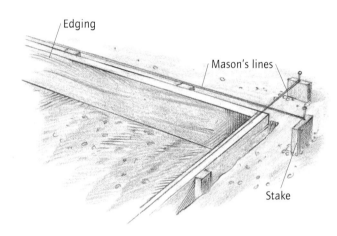

2. To assemble the patio, string mason's line from stakes outside the corners to serve as guides for installing the edgings at the correct level. The edgings also serve as leveling guides for sand and bricks.

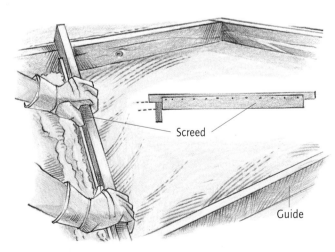

3. Lay down a 1½- to 2-inch layer of dampened sand and level it with a bladed screed, as shown. If the patio is too wide for the screed, rest one end on a temporary guide.

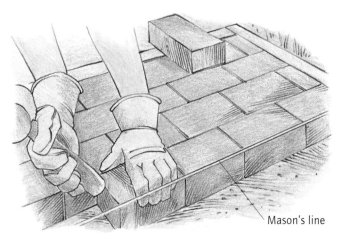

4. Another mason's line will help align brick courses. Beginning at one corner, lay bricks tightly against one another, tapping each into place with a hand sledge or mallet. Check level frequently.

Concrete pavers can be laid in sand in much the same way bricks are. Interlocking pavers are especially easy to lay, because the alignment between the units is almost automatic. After laying these units, settle them with a vibrating plate compactor or a drum roller. Then spread damp fine sand over the surface; when the sand dries, sweep it into the paver joints. Additional passes with the vibrator or roller will help lock the pavers together.

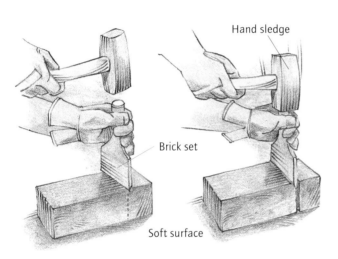

5. To cut bricks by hand, use a brick set to score a line on all 4 sides (left); make the cut with one sharp blow (right). Wear gloves and protective goggles.

6. Throw damp fine sand over the finished pavement and let it dry for a few hours. Then, with a stiff broom, sweep sand into the joints. Spray with water so that sand settles completely.

Brick Patterns

When choosing a brick pattern (also known as a bond), consider the degree of difficulty involved in laying it. Some bonds require not only accuracy, but also a lot of brick cutting. The patterns shown below are some of the most popular; the jack-on-jack and running bonds are the simplest to lay.

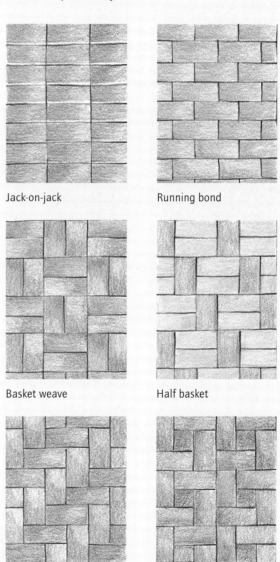

Jack-on-jack

Running bond

Basket weave

Half basket

Herringbone

Pinwheel

Laying Flagstone in Mortar

The instructions below show you how to lay flagstone in mortar, but they are applicable to any masonry unit—brick, broken concrete, or ceramic tile—that you wish to set in mortar. Be sure to allow a minimum slope for drainage off a path. One-quarter inch of slope per foot of width (measure from center to edge on each side) makes a crowned path that sheds water quickly.

For the most permanent masonry surface, set stone, bricks, or tiles in a mortar bed over concrete that is at least 3 inches thick. If you're building on an existing slab, it must be clean and in good condition. Ask a concrete dealer whether you need to apply a bonding agent for mortar on either an existing or new concrete surface.

Mixing Mortar

Mortar recipes vary according to their intended use, but the ingredients are usually the same: portland cement, sand, in some cases lime (or fireclay), and water. You can either make your own or buy more expensive ready-to-mix mortar. To build a wall, you'll need a mix of 1 part cement, $\frac{1}{2}$ part hydrated lime or fireclay, and 6 parts sand. This mixture is much like Type N mortar, commonly sold for general use. In contrast, a typical mortar for paving and most other below-grade installations contains only 1 part portland cement and 3 parts sand.

Small amounts of mortar can easily be mixed by hand. Note that mortar is caustic, so wear gloves when you work with it. Measure the sand, cement, and lime

Mortar bag

1. Dry-fit all stones, trimming, if necessary. Then prepare a mortar mix just stiff enough to support the stones, yet wet enough to stick. Spread mortar at least 1 inch deep, covering enough space to lay 1 or 2 stones at a time. Make furrows in the mortar with a trowel.

2. Set each stone in place, bedding it with a rubber mallet and checking for level. If a stone isn't level, lift it up and scoop out or add mortar as needed. Clean stones with a wet cloth as you work.

3. Let mortar set for 24 hours, then grout joints with the same mortar mix (plus an optional $\frac{1}{2}$ to 1 part fireclay for workability, but no lime). A mortar bag keeps mortar off stones that might stain.

(if used) into a wheelbarrow or similar container. Use a hoe to mix the dry ingredients thoroughly and form them into a pile. Make a depression in the center of the dry ingredients and pour in some water. Mix, then repeat the process, adding water gradually until the mortar has a smooth, uniform, granular consistency, spreads well, and adheres to vertical surfaces but does not "smear" the face of your work (an indication that it's too watery). Mix only enough mortar to last a few hours; any more is likely to be wasted.

Trimming Stone

Because most flagstones are irregular, you'll probably need to trim some pieces before setting them. Wear gloves and safety glasses even for minor trimming jobs. Chip off small pieces with a mason's hammer or brick set and hand sledge. To make a major cut, use the adjacent stone as a guide and proceed with a brick set and sledge, as shown at right.

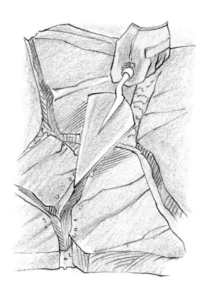

4. If the stone is a nonstaining type, you can work grout across stones into joints with a wet sponge. No matter how the grout is applied, use a mason's trowel to smooth the joints.

TRIMMING STONE

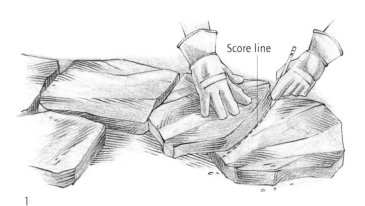

Score line

1

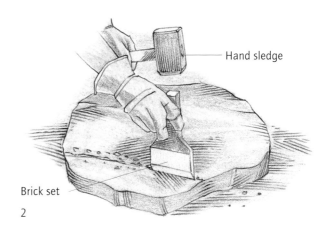

Hand sledge

Brick set

2

Break over scrap wood

3

To cut flagstone, lay one block over its neighbor and trace its outline (1). Then score a groove in the stone to be cut (2). Finally, prop up the stone and split it with a sharp blow (3).

Courtyards

A courtyard is a transitional space. Enclosed by walls, it's part garden, part house, offering privacy, open air, plantings, and furnishings—and thanks to the walls, it has a more intimate, romantic feeling than a simple patio or deck. An openwork gate provides a tantalizing look inside; a solid one heightens the feeling of privacy for those within. On smaller properties, a courtyard may be designed as the entrance to a townhouse; it can also form the entire garden for an urban lot.

Water features, especially fountains, are particularly at home in a courtyard. Decorate the walls with vines, set out pots or planters of fragrant flowers, add subtle night lighting, and your courtyard becomes a haven. If space allows, install a fireplace to give welcome warmth in chilly weather, making outdoor entertaining a pleasure.

Courtyard floors are typically constructed from the same types of material as terraces and patios. Brick, pavers, concrete, stone, tile, and even gravel can all be used to good effect. Choose a material and pattern to complement your house and other elements of the courtyard.

As in other aspects of garden design, keep scale in mind. A huge courtyard beside a small house looks out of place, as does a tiny one in front of a regal entryway. Try to match your plantings to both courtyard and house, perhaps choosing paired plantings (such as mirror-image potted roses or other shrubs) for formal homes and asymmetrical, informal arrangements for more contemporary designs. Entry courtyards are viewed throughout the year, so remember to vary plantings and accessories for all-season interest.

ABOVE *Cloaked in greenery, this intimate walled courtyard lies just beyond a master bath suite. Evergreen creeping fig coats the wall and surrounds the fountain. Wisteria, trained to a wire trellis bolted into the top of the wall, adds more privacy.*

LEFT *An elegant gateway opens onto this entry courtyard, which has a dining area just the right size for a small gathering. The floor and walls are made of mortared bricks in several hues.*

Fireplaces

An outdoor fireplace makes a great gathering spot. It creates a feeling of intimacy while letting you and your guests stay outdoors even on cool evenings. You can install the fireplace in a sheltered entry courtyard, along the rear wall of the house, or at the boundary between paved and planted areas. While wood is the usual fuel, many homeowners opt for natural gas, which is safer and cleaner.

Outdoor fireplaces contain all the basic elements of indoor ones: a center firebox, with a back wall that reflects the radiant energy of the fire outward; and a chimney, which improves the draw and lifts smoke above roof height. Check with your local building department for regulations on fireplace location, construction, and chimney height.

Traditional masonry fireplaces have a footing, a firebrick-lined firebox, and a brick-lined or stone chimney. A lighter, less expensive choice is a zero-clearance unit, which can be installed in contact with combustible framing material; it has a prefabricated metal shell and a metal chimney. The unit is framed with studs, encased in plywood or backerboard, and finished with stone, stucco, or tile.

There are also precast modules (made of pumice stone or cast concrete) that stack together to make the firebox, fireplace, and chimney. Installing these lighter-weight sections is easier than dealing with heavy solid units. Or opt for a simple, portable metal firepit; available models include kinds that burn propane or natural gas, as well as wood-burning sorts. Be sure to locate any firepit at a safe distance from structures, on a nonflammable surface well away from overhanging trees and other vegetation; outfit it with a screened cover to keep sparks under control.

ABOVE *A beautiful focal point for the garden, this freestanding limestone fireplace makes sitting outside enjoyable even when the weather turns cool.*

BELOW *Guests enjoy gathering around this large fireplace, enhanced with pots, decorative objects, and a tracery of creeping fig.*

Paths and Steps

All gardens have paths of one sort or another. A front walkway beckons visitors toward the house, while a winding trail invites them to explore the garden. Other paths serve mainly practical purposes, such as providing access to a side yard or garden shed.

Match the materials to the path's intended use. Walks for major access should be made of formed or stamped concrete, brick, pavers, or stone slabs—materials that allow easy traffic flow and provide an even, nonskid surface. By contrast, wood chips and gravel work beautifully for rustic paths that meander through the garden; the uneven texture and natural colors blend seamlessly into the surroundings. Rough cobbles, salvaged bricks, and other casual stepping-stones also make appealing paths, especially when embedded in contrasting materials such as gravel, sand, or wood chips. Grass paths are another choice; they look quite elegant when neatly clipped and bordered by sweeps of ground cover or mulched planting beds.

How wide should your path be? Again, it depends on the intended purpose. If the path will wind dis-

ABOVE *Salvaged bricks, streaked with old mortar, are set into this casual path to give it a soft, aged appearance.*

creetly through the garden and serve only as a walking surface, a width of 2 feet is adequate. To allow room for lawn mowers and wheelbarrows, make it 3 feet wide. For an entry path that will allow two people to walk abreast, aim for a width of 4 to 5 feet.

Steps serve a practical function as transitions between different levels of the garden, but they can serve as accents, too. Most dramatic are wide, deep steps that lead the eye to a garden focal point. Good-sized steps can also double as retaining walls, planters, or garden seating.

As is the case with paths, materials influence the style of steps. Poured concrete, masonry units, and concrete pavers usually present a substantial, somewhat formal look. Natural materials such as stone, on the other hand, have an informal style and suit less structured gardens.

Regardless of the material you use, put safety first. Treads should give safe footing in wet weather, and night lighting should be bright enough to let you go up and down without tripping (you can use unobtrusive path lights or built-in fixtures).

LEFT *Exuberant plantings of ferns, shrubs, and ornamental grasses soften a flight of stone steps.*

ABOVE *Bricks offer many possibilities for paths. You can mortar them onto a cement slab or lay them in sand, and arrange them in a number of patterns (see pages 110–111).*

RIGHT *The paving makes this straight, stepped walkway distinctive. One-foot squares of lilac Pennsylvania stone, laid diagonally, are bordered by rectangles of the same stone.*

117

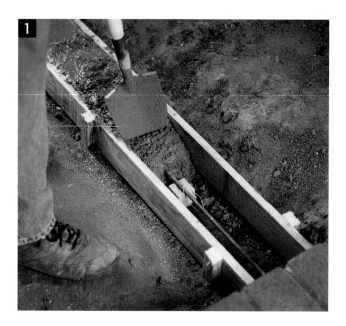

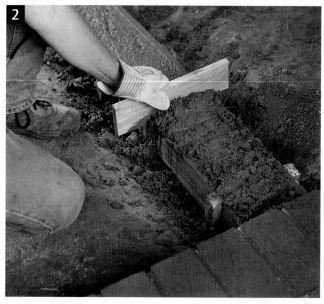

Installing a Gravel Path with a Brick Border

Gravel makes low-cost, fast-draining paths that suit a wide variety of formal and informal garden styles. You can opt for pea gravel or the more stable crushed rock; adding flagstones gives a firmer walking surface. An edging serves to keep the gravel in place—and it looks attractive, too. Shown here is brick mortared onto a concrete footing; you could also use lumber, stacked concrete retaining blocks, or manufactured plastic or metal edgings.

1 *Before building the forms for the footing, excavate the path area (plus 6 inches on either side to provide working space) to a depth of 4 inches. (In areas where the soil freezes, you may need to excavate deeper and add a layer of gravel to help prevent frost heaving; consult your local building department for advice.) Tamp the soil to make it firm and level.*

Construct the forms from 2 by 4s; hold them in place with 1-by-2 stakes along the outside edges. Check often to be sure the forms are level as you work. Place rebar down the middle of the forms; the wires embedded in dobies—small blocks of precast concrete—hold the rebar in place. Mix the concrete (see page 107) and shovel it into the forms.

2 *Screed (level) the concrete by moving a board along the tops of the forms with a sawing motion. When the concrete is*

set, remove the forms. To cure the concrete, keep it damp for 3 to 7 days by covering it with plastic sheeting or sprinkling it frequently.

3 *To aid in aligning the bricks, run mason's line along the outside edge of the concrete border at the height of one brick; also check the level often with a carpenter's level. Wet bricks so they won't suck moisture from the mortar. Mix mortar (see page 112) and spread a ½-inch-thick layer over the concrete, enough to lay 3 or 4 bricks. Set the first brick in place on the mortar. "Butter" the end of the next brick with mortar and join it to the first brick; the mortar joint should be about ½ inch thick. Continue in this way until the border is complete. If you need to cut bricks to fit, see page 111 for directions.*

4 *Lay landscape fabric over the path area between the borders to prevent weed growth. Spread 2 inches of dampened sand on the fabric. Tamp the sand to make it level and firm, sprinkling lightly with water as you work.*

5 *Add about ½ inch more sand to accept the flagstones (don't tamp it down). Set the flagstones in the sand; they should be ½ to ¾ inch higher than the finished path (the added height helps keep gravel off the stones). If necessary, add or remove sand to adjust the height of the flagstones and prevent wobbling. Spread gravel over the path and rake it smooth around the stones.*

Step-building Basics

Well-designed steps have good proportions: the height of the risers (the vertical part of the steps) relative to the depth of the treads (the horizontal part) allows for comfortable climbing. The shorter the riser, the deeper the tread should be; conversely, the taller the riser, the shallower the tread. A handy formula for figuring a good riser-tread ratio for most outdoor steps is to make sure that twice the riser height plus the depth of the tread (in inches) equals 26; for example, a riser height of 5 inches would call for a tread depth of 16 inches (see the chart below for more examples). Some landscape designers incorporate wiggle room into the equation by expressing the total as a range of 25 to 27 inches.

For maximum comfort in climbing the steps, plan to make the riser no lower than 4 inches and no higher than 7 inches; the middle range (5 to 6 inches) is considered ideal. For safety's sake, make all the steps in any one stairway uniform in size.

To construct a stairway between two fixed points, begin by calculating the change in level between those points. Measure the height of the slope (A to B in the drawing) as well as the horizontal distance, or run (A to C). To decide how many steps you will need, divide the desired riser height into the slope height (in inches); drop any fractional remainder. Now find the corresponding tread size on the riser-tread relationship chart. To determine whether the steps will fit into the run, multiply the tread size by the number of steps. For a proper fit,

Thanks to carefully placed low-voltage lights, these blue-stone steps are well lit at night.

the resulting number should be approximately equal to the run from A to C.

Sometimes steps of the proportions you want won't fit the slope exactly. You may be able to make them fit by adjusting riser and tread dimensions slightly; or you may have to cut and fill the slope to accommodate the steps. If the slope is too steep even for 7-inch risers, remember that an outdoor stairway need not run straight up and down; you can make use of curves, switchbacks, and even landings.

Plan on a minimum width of 2 feet for utility steps and 4 feet for most others. If you want two people to be able to walk abreast, allow 5 feet. Also plan to make the steps at least as wide as the path that leads to them. Note that broad steps allow you to incorporate seating and planters.

For safety, steps leading to porches or decks should have at least one handrail. Also plan to install outdoor lighting fixtures; you can tie them into the normal household wiring or use easy-to-install low-voltage lighting.

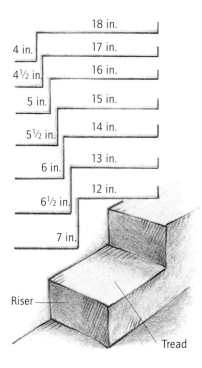

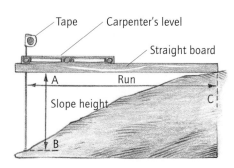

Stone Steps

Wide, flat stones make beautifully natural-looking steps that work especially well in informal areas of the garden or wherever foot traffic isn't high. It's easiest to construct these steps without mortar, but to do so, you will need quite large, heavy, stable stones—about 20 inches deep, 2 feet wide, and 6 to 8 inches thick.

Starting at the downhill end of the slope, excavate a hole for the first stone. Spread 2 inches of sand over the bottom of the hole (if your soil drains poorly, dig deeper and spread 4 inches of gravel beneath the sand). Dampen and tamp the sand; then lay the stone in place and twist it until it's level and firmly embedded.

With the first stone securely in place, position the next one, working up the slope; overlap the stones a few inches for stability. (If necessary, cushion each stone with a layer of sand to help seat it firmly.) For extra strength, you can spread a 1-inch-thick layer of mortar (see page 112) at the back of each step before adding the next, to bond the steps together where they meet.

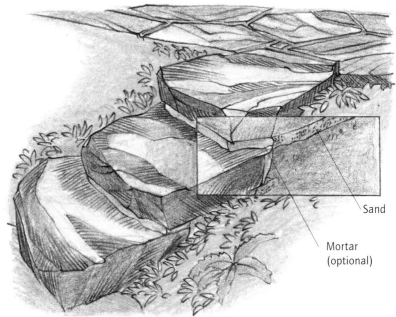

Sand

Mortar (optional)

Tie or Timber Steps

Both railroad ties and 6-by-6 pressure-treated landscape timbers make simple, rugged steps. Excavate the site to accommodate the shape of the steps, firmly tamping the soil. After cutting the lumber to the proper length, drill a hole near each end. Lay the risers in place on the stairway, check for level, and use a sledge to drive either $1/2$-inch galvanized steel pipes or $3/4$-inch reinforcing bars through the holes into the ground. Or, for extra support, pour small concrete footings; let the concrete stiffen slightly, then set anchor bolts in it. When the concrete is set (after about 2 days), secure the ties or timbers to the footing with the bolts.

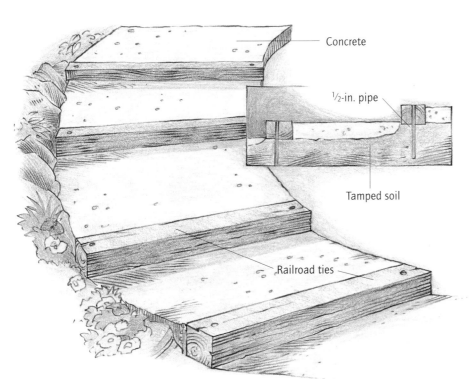

Concrete

$1/2$-in. pipe

Tamped soil

Railroad ties

Walls

Walls define space, provide privacy and security, edit views, screen out wind and noise, and hold the earth at bay. They bring an unmatched sense of permanence to a garden; in fact, some of the world's oldest structures are walls. Once you've determined a wall's function, you can choose its exact location, height, width, and degree of visual permeability. You'll also need to select materials that coordinate with the style and design of your house and existing garden structures.

Before beginning any wall, check with your local building department for relevant regulations. There may be rules involving how close to your property line and how high you can build; what kind of foundation you'll need; and whether or not the wall requires steel reinforcement. Many municipalities require a building permit for any masonry wall more than 3 feet high.

Materials for garden walls include brick, concrete blocks, stackable retaining blocks, poured concrete, and uncut stone. *Brick* and *concrete blocks* are easiest to work with, since they're units of uniform size that you assemble piece by piece. You can choose a decorative pattern for laying the courses, incorporate a solid or openwork face, vary the wall's thickness, and employ combinations of materials. *Poured concrete,* too, offers many design possibilities: the surface texture and shape can vary widely, depending on the forms you use. *Stone* creates walls that seem to be part of the landscape; native stone, of course, looks the most natural.

A BASIC BRICK WALL

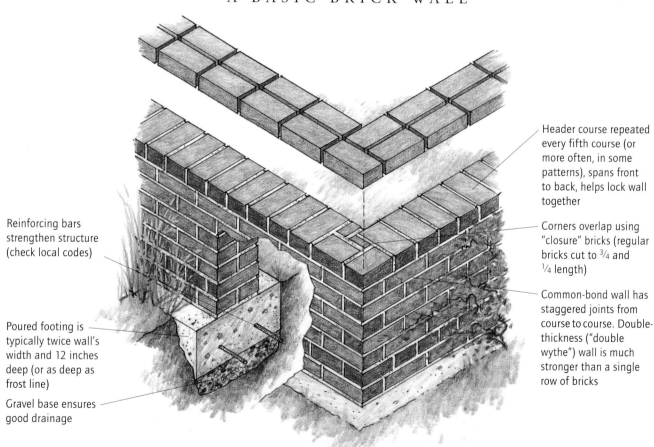

Header course repeated every fifth course (or more often, in some patterns), spans front to back, helps lock wall together

Corners overlap using "closure" bricks (regular bricks cut to ³/₄ and ¹/₄ length)

Common-bond wall has staggered joints from course to course. Double-thickness ("double wythe") wall is much stronger than a single row of bricks

Reinforcing bars strengthen structure (check local codes)

Poured footing is typically twice wall's width and 12 inches deep (or as deep as frost line)

Gravel base ensures good drainage

Build a Dry Stone Wall

Building a Dry Stone Wall

The key to a successful dry stone wall is careful fitting—and some hard work. Constructed with little or no mortar, these walls owe their stability to the weight and friction of one stone against another. When properly placed, the stones should look almost like single unit—certainly not just a pile of rocks.

Dry stone walls are usually laid in two rough wythes (rows), with rubble fill between them. Bond stones run across the wall from side to side, tying it together. Use as many bond stones as possible—at least one every 2 to 3 feet. As you work, be sure that vertical joints are staggered. Keep in mind the stonemason's rule: One stone over two, two over one.

Dry stone walls should slope inward on both sides. This tilting, called "batter," helps secure the wall, since the faces lean on each other. A good rule of thumb is to plan 3 to 4 inches of batter for each 2 feet of rise. To check your work, make a batter gauge (shown above) from a carpenter's level, a straight 2 by 2 or 2 by 4, and a scrap of 2 by 2.

1 *Dig a trench and lay the first stones. Remove sod and other organic matter from an area about 3 inches wider than the desired bottom thickness of the wall. Scrape rather than dig the bottom of the depression, so stones will rest on undisturbed soil. Lay a bond stone at either end; then lay stones in 2 wythes between the bond stones. Tightly pack small stones between the wythes to fill in the space.*

2 *Lay additional courses. Aim to make the courses fairly level. Use your batter gauge to be sure that the wall leans in slightly on both sides. Every third or fourth course, install bond stones every 2 to 3 feet. If you need to cut stones, see page 113.*

3 *Finish the wall. Fill any large gaps in the wall by gently tapping in small stones. Finish the top with large, flat cap-stones that overhang the sides of the wall on either side. For a stronger wall, lay the capstones in a 1- to 2-inch-thick bed of mortar (see page 112).*

Retaining Walls and Raised Beds

Garden structures designed to hold soil in place include retaining walls, which can range from simple piles of stones to tall concrete barriers, and raised beds or boxes. Raised beds do more than simply hold soil, of course—they're planting beds and can be design features, too.

Retaining Walls

Unlike freestanding garden walls, retaining walls must withstand the force of earth pushing against them. Depending on the steepness of the slope and the height of the wall, that pressure can be tremendous, especially when heavy rains and melting snow saturate the soil. That's why careful planning is important in the siting, design, and construction of a retaining wall.

Simple, low retaining walls on gently sloping, stable ground are manageable do-it-yourself projects. You may want to install a single wall at the base of a slope, or terrace the slope with a series of walls. For a tall wall or where extensive grading is required, or where the

A low retaining wall of dry-stacked stone gains color and texture from small plants that grow in the crevices between the rocks.

ground is unstable or steep, you'll need to call in a professional—usually a licensed engineer or landscape contractor. In any case, it's important to consult your local building department, as most communities require a building permit for any retaining wall.

Stackable Retaining Blocks

Traditional materials for retaining walls include wood, stone, and poured concrete. More recently, various styles of modular, stackable, interlocking concrete blocks have been developed; these offer an easy way for a homeowner to build a low retaining wall or raised bed. Most interlocking blocks have a lip at the rear bottom that slips over the top back edge of the block below. Others are anchored with grooves or fiberglass pins. All are installed without using mortar.

To build a wall with these blocks, begin by laying out the site and doing any necessary slope excavation. Then dig a trench 6 inches wider and 6 inches deeper than the width of your blocks. Fill the trench with compactible gravel and tamp. Lay the blocks, following the manufacturer's directions and filling in behind the wall with gravel as you go.

Each of these stackable retaining blocks has a lip that slips over the back of the block below and interlocks with it. The top course, shown here, is secured with construction adhesive.

Raised Beds

Raised beds are a perfect place for herbs, vegetables, or flowers for cutting. Because you can fill them with the good, fast-draining soil that many plants prefer, they're especially useful where native soil is poor and/or compacted. Raised beds also make it possible to care for plants and to harvest vegetables without stooping. Line the bottom of the bed with aviary wire to keep out burrowing pests such as gophers, or with landscape fabric to reduce root invasion from nearby trees (or use both wire and landscape fabric, if needed).

You can design your own raised bed or purchase a kit from a garden supply company. Many gardeners like to use rot-resistant lumber, as shown here; if you opt for pressure-treated lumber, line the inside of the bed with heavy polyethylene to prevent chemicals from leaching into the soil. Other choices include long-lasting plastic or composite lumber (see page 85) and stackable retaining blocks.

For the raised bed shown here, you'll need six 4 by 6s, 8 feet long; one 2 by 2, 12 feet long; and two 2 by 6s, 8 feet long. We give directions for building one box, but you can easily extend your garden by building more raised beds.

A RAISED-BOX PLANTER

1. For the sides of the box, cut each 4 by 6 in half to make a total of twelve 4-foot-long pieces. Cut the 2 by 2 into eight pieces, each 1½ feet long. To make caps for the box, cut both 2 by 6s in half, making the cuts at a 45° angle. Then cut the square ends of the resulting 4 pieces of 2 by 6 at a 45° angle.

2. Stack the 4 by 6s with joints overlapping, as shown at below. To hold the box together, attach the 1½-foot-long pieces of 2 by 2 to each interior corner and middle of each side, using

wood screws. Lay the 2-by-6 cap pieces in place, with their inner edges even with the inner edges of the box. Attach the 2 by 2s to the caps with wood screws. To reinforce cap, screw cap boards to 4 by 6s below.

3. Install the box in a level spot. If desired, cover the ground under the box with landscape fabric and/or aviary wire. Fill with good, fast-draining soil; then set in plants.

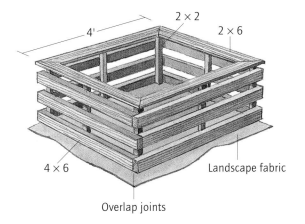

4'   2 × 2   2 × 6

4 × 6   Landscape fabric

Overlap joints

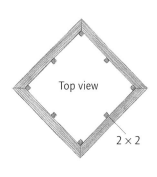

Top view

2 × 2

Water Features

A wall-mounted fountain, a lily pond, a rushing waterfall—in any form, a water feature transforms the landscape, making the garden more attractive to both people and wildlife. The sound of falling water masks traffic noise and other neighborhood hubbub, creating a sense of peace and tranquillity.

A pleasing water feature can be as modest as a spill fountain in a ceramic urn or as elaborate as a stone sculpture that sends a graceful arc of water into a large pond or pool.

Many gardeners opt for a pond, complete with fish and aquatic plants. Site the pond carefully: don't choose a low-lying area that will be inundated in wet weather, and don't build too close to deciduous trees that may cast too much shade over the pond in spring and summer or shed leaves and twigs into the water in autumn. If you want to raise plants and fish in the pond, keep in mind that the minimum pond depth is about 1½ feet. Small ponds can be installed using a rigid pre-formed shell; larger ones are usually made with a thick, flexible pool liner (see pages 128–129).

You can incorporate a spray fountain or waterfall into any type of pond. Spray fountains use assorted heads that shoot water in tall columns or make a lacy mist. Waterfalls send a cascade toward the pond from a simple outlet pipe. Both features use a submersible pump; most operate on household electricity, though some smaller fountains run on solar power. Check with an electrician or your local building department before running electricity to your pond, and be sure to verify safety requirements for pond placement and depth.

TOP *Birds are drawn to the soft splash of a little spill fountain set in rocks over an underground basin.*

LEFT *A handsome fountain marks the intersection of brick-edged gravel paths in this garden of roses and herbs.*

ABOVE *Straight lines and careful masonry work give this pond and the surrounding walkways a formal air. A pond rimmed with stones, in contrast, would appear more rustic.*

RIGHT *Flowing over native stone and surrounded by casual plantings, this cascading waterfall blends naturally into the hillside.*

BELOW *A classical feature such as this cherub fountain effectively dresses up an elegant swimming pool.*

Installing a Garden Pond with a Flexible Liner

A flexible synthetic rubber liner allows you to design a pond in almost any shape, letting you make a natural-looking pool with curves that mimic those you'd see in the wild. Flexible liners are relatively easy to install, conform readily to your excavation, and can make fairly large ponds—unlike rigid-shell liners, which are typically small and require that you match your excavation precisely to their shape.

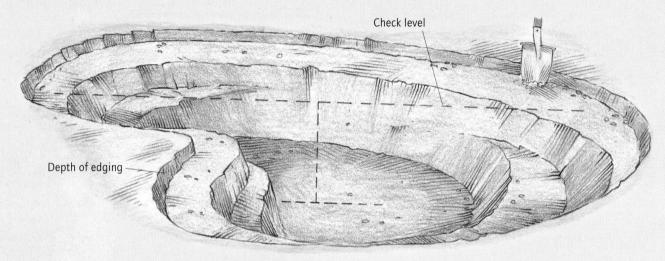

Check level

Depth of edging

1. Mark the pond's outline with a hose or length of rope. Dig all around the outline with a sharp spade. Excavate the hole, allowing for edging material (such as flat stones) and, if desired, shelves for aquatic plants; dig out an extra 2 inches for a layer of sand. Check for level, using a straight board to bridge the rim.

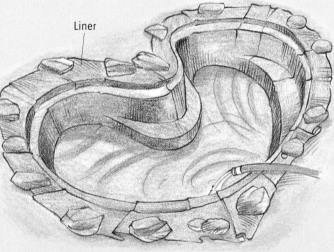

Liner

3. Open up the liner and let it soften in the sun. Then spread it over the hole, evening up the overlap all around; a helper makes this step much easier. Place stones around the perimeter to hold the liner in place. Begin to fill the pond slowly with water; the weight of the water helps the liner conform to the contours of the excavation.

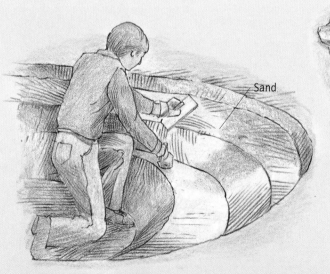

Sand

2. Remove all protruding roots and rocks and fill holes with soil. Pack a 2-inch layer of damp sand into the excavation; the sand helps protect the liner from any sharp rocks hidden just under the surface. Smooth the sand with a board or a concrete float.

Tuck in wrinkles

4. Continue filling, smoothing the liner and creasing it, as needed. Fold the liner into pleats at any hard corners (the folds won't be visible once the pool is filled).

5. When the pond is full, add an edging of flat stones, extending them about 2 inches over the lip of the pond to help hide the liner. If you add several courses of stones, offset them so that the joints are not aligned. If desired, mortar the stones in place (see page 112). Finally, trim off any extra liner.

Fountains and Waterfalls

Water in motion is an enchanting addition to the garden. Both fountains and waterfalls depend on submersible pumps to circulate water. Such pumps are usually connected to the main household electrical supply, but low-voltage pumps are also available. These require a simple transformer that steps down 120-volt power to a safe 12 volts; the transformer itself plugs into a 120-volt outlet, which must be protected by a GFCI (ground fault circuit interrupter) if it's located outdoors. You can also buy solar-powered pumps, which don't need any wiring.

Fountain styles vary widely. For a patio or as a focal point in the garden, consider a fountain installed in a single pot or in a stack of containers. A bubbler or spray feature (see bottom photo on page 126) creates movement and sound. Spill fountains allow water to trickle or sheet over the pot's sides into a hidden reser-

voir beneath it, then recirculate the water back into the container. In wall fountains, a stream or spray of water tumbles into a basin or pool below. The holding reservoir is often raised above ground level; it's usually made of concrete or concrete blocks and faced with some other type of masonry material, such as brick, tile, or stone. Home supply centers offer some choices for fountains and pumps, but you'll find a wider selection in shops that specialize in water gardens.

A simple waterfall can splash directly into one end of a pond; place a submersible pump in the pond and hide the water supply tube behind a layer of rocks. Stack more rocks to make the waterfall, placing the supply tube among them. In more complex waterfalls, the water first plunges into a stream or channel, then may ripple over a series of rocks before falling into a pond. To make a waterproof channel, use a flexible liner, free-form concrete, a fiberglass shell, a series of splash pans, or a combination of these options.

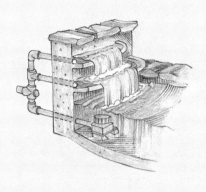

A formal wall fountain combines a raised holding pool, masonry wall, and decorative spill shelves. Water tumbles from pipe outlets to spill shelves to the holding pool; a submersible pump sends the water back around again.

This simple waterfall spills into a pond. Place a submersible pump in the pond and camouflage its tubing behind rocks. By adjusting the control on the pump and rearranging rocks, you can easily vary the flow of water and its sound.

Plant Palette

I perhaps owe having become a painter to flowers.

—Claude Monet

Trees

Wherever you live in the South and whatever garden style you prefer, you'll find there's no more important landscape component than trees. For starters, their impact is enormous—not just for size, but also for the practical and aesthetic values they bring to the garden. On the practical side, trees offer shade from intense sun and shelter from wind, both of which enhance your comfort and, very likely, reduce your home's energy consumption. Aesthetically, trees serve a variety of purposes. First and foremost, they establish scale; depending on your tree choices (or the trees already growing on the site), they can frame a house or garden or tower over the landscape. Trees can conceal unsightly features—both on your property and beyond it—and they can be strategically placed to draw the eye toward attractive vistas. Often, trees are planted for their individual beauty, to be cherished for their colorful flowers, seasonal foliage color, or simple elegance of form.

One frequently overlooked value of trees is their ability to give a garden the air of permanence. Nothing moderates the starkness of a new housing development better than trees as they grow to soften and nestle the homes. A mature tree suggests *forever*. In fact, the stately trees that grace your neighborhood may well be heritage plants—legacies from previous generations of gardeners.

Selecting the Right Tree

As you begin to consider tree choices for your garden, first determine what you want to accomplish. Do you need a shade-maker for your yard? Choose a tree that develops a sizable foliage canopy—tall or wide-spreading (or both), depending on the area to be shaded. If you need to hide an eyesore or simply establish privacy, you may want an evergreen that keeps its foliage all the way to the ground and year-round. Perhaps you want a focal point. Then look for a tree that offers striking form, attractive bark, or colorful

ABOVE *In autumn, red maple (*Acer rubrum *'October Glory') ignites in spectacular color.*

INSET *Clouds of bloom cover a native flowering dogwood in spring.*

flowers or foliage. Once you've established the effect you want, you can begin narrowing your field of choices.

The most basic distinction between trees is whether they are deciduous or evergreen. Deciduous trees (see page 135) are bare of foliage during winter, then sprout leaves in spring and carry them throughout summer; in fall, the leaves may turn a brilliant color before they drop. Evergreen trees (see page 134), on the other hand, retain their foliage year-round, even though they may don some new leaves in spring and drop the oldest leaves a few at a time during the course of the year. These "always green" trees are ideal for screens or as points of interest during winter months. You can choose from two kinds: broad-leafed evergreens, such as Southern magnolia and most hollies, with leaf forms similar to those of deciduous trees;

TREE SILHOUETTES

Columnar	Oval	Pyramidal	Rounded	Vase-shaped	Weeping

and coniferous evergreens, so-called because they all bear some sort of cone as a fruit. Among conifers, there are two types. Needle-leafed sorts, such as pines and cedars, sport narrow, needlelike leaves; scale-leafed kinds, like the cypresses, bear foliage sprays composed of tiny scales.

Once you've decided between deciduous or evergreen, consider the tree's growth rate and ultimate size. A desire for quick shade or instant privacy may tempt you to buy a fast-growing species such as silver maple or cottonwood, but such a vigorous tree has drawbacks. Roots may crack sidewalks and invade water lines; weak wood may break easily in storms; and the tree's sheer size may overwhelm the area, especially if it's planted too near the house. Instant gratification may lead to costly damage, removal, and replacement some years later.

Consider, too, a tree's mature shape, which may not be obvious when you buy a small sapling at the nursery. A vase-shaped type, such as Japanese zelkova, for example, makes a good choice for a lawn or street tree because the ascending branches leave plenty of headroom underneath. Rounded, spreading trees (such as live oak and Norway maple) need lots of horizontal space in which to extend their branches. Columnar trees, such as 'Columnare' red maple and various conifers, don't require much elbow room and work well where space is restricted.

Many trees offer a spectacular burst of color in fall, but some also give you variations on standard-issue green during spring and summer. You'll find deciduous trees with golden, bronzy, red, or bluish green summer foliage; and among evergreens, especially

coniferous types, you can also find an assortment of colored-foliage choices. All of these make striking focal points but should be used sparingly to avoid creating a jumble of colors.

PLANTING TREES

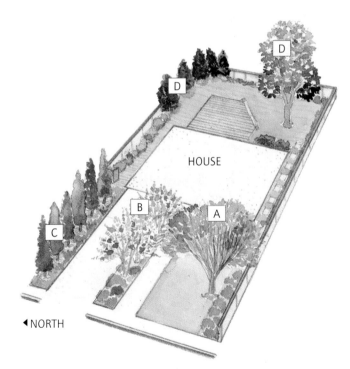

◄ NORTH

A. Mature deciduous trees lend an established look, and shade the front of the house in summer.

B. Flowering trees in bloom add color to front entryway.

C. Needle-leafed evergreens screen the driveway from view year-round.

D. Broad-leafed evergreens offer privacy and shade without excessive leaf litter.

Evergreen Trees

Among trees, evergreens are the mainstays of Southern gardens because they suit so many needs. With their year-round foliage, they lend constant, permanent structure and visual weight to the landscape. They also add color and interest in wintertime, when deciduous trees are leafless. From spring through fall, evergreens can fill background roles to show off special flowering trees and shrubs, serve as useful windbreaks and tall screens, or simply provide welcome shade.

Coniferous evergreens (both needle- and scale-leafed) include American arborvitae *(Thuja occidentalis)*, eastern red cedar *(Juniperus virginiana)*, hemlock *(Tsuga)*, Leyland cypress (× *Cupressocyparis leylandii)*, pine *(Pinus)*, spruce *(Picea)*, and true cedar *(Cedrus)*.

Common broad-leafed evergreens include American holly *(Ilex opaca)*, Carolina cherry laurel *(Prunus caroliniana)*, glossy privet *(Ligustrum lucidum)*, live oak *(Quercus virginiana)*, palms (see pages 138–139), and Southern magnolia *(Magnolia grandiflora)*.

Though evergreens may seem a panacea for your landscaping needs, these trees do have some faults. Chief among these is the dense shade they cast, which makes it difficult to grow lawn grass beneath them. And because many have a low branching structure that allows little to no headroom beneath, they often are not the best choices for planting along a street or in a courtyard. You can always remove the lower branches, though doing so may sacrifice the natural form and beauty of many trees, particularly conifers. (Pines are a notable exception, because most of them naturally drop their lower limbs as they grow.) Because evergreen trees tend to dominate a garden, they should be used judiciously. Planting them in quantity produces a gloomy, overly shady garden better suited to growing mushrooms than colorful flowering plants. To these objectionable traits you can also add messiness. Many evergreens shed leaves, needles, cones, and/or seeds throughout the year, while deciduous trees drop leaves and most other litter just once, in the fall.

TOP *Southern magnolia* (Magnolia grandiflora) *is the South's favorite evergreen tree. Sizes vary (smaller and larger forms are sold) but shallow roots make them poor lawn trees.*

ABOVE *A threadleaf Sawara false cypress* (Chamaecyparis pisifera 'Filifera Aurea') *presents a golden spire of cascading foliage year-round.*

Deciduous Trees

In much of the South, from mountains to lowlands, deciduous trees are part of nature's landscape—so much so, in fact, that it's easy to take them for granted. Where homes are built in naturally wooded regions, deciduous trees may automatically and instantly become the basic foundation or "bones" of the garden-to-be. In contrast to evergreens, these trees drop their leaves once in fall and refoliate after winter has passed. This leafy-to-bare cycle offers a set of unique advantages.

In a nutshell, deciduous trees give your garden seasonal change. At some near-magical point at the end of winter, bare limbs sprout a haze of new growth which quickly becomes a verdant cloak of fresh leaves. Flowers may be part of the equation in spring (before or with the new leaves) or in summer, though many choice deciduous types have earned stellar reputations even without a floral display. In the fullness of summer, deciduous trees look lush and bursting with life. But it is toward the end of their growing season when most deciduous trees command attention—at the moment when their leaves change to autumnal shades of yellow, gold, orange, red, or maroon before dropping from the branches.

Many deciduous trees are excellent choices for garden or patio. They provide shade during the warmest months but graciously drop their leaves in fall to let warming winter sun shine through their framework of bare branches. By strategically locating deciduous trees to cool the house in summer and *not* cool it in winter, you can achieve an energy saving which translates to reduced heating and cooling costs.

Among deciduous trees, you'll find a wide variety of shapes and sizes; some give you dense foliage canopies, while others are fetchingly see-through. But don't judge by beauty alone—be sure to coordinate a tree's characteristics to the role it will play in your landscape. Be prepared for fall leaf cleanup, but consider it a small price to pay for the varied benefits these trees offer throughout the year.

From its early spring leaf-out to its flaming finish in autumn, Amur maple (Acer tataricum ginnala) is a stellar small tree, suited to a variety of soils and climates.

Tree Care

Thinning. *Selectively thin the branches of a shade tree to prevent the tree from forming an overly dense canopy; this will reduce the likelihood of wind damage, and, in the process, open up "windows" to views. Remove weak limbs and vertical-growing water sprouts at their point of origin first, along with any branches that rub or cross one another. Clear out branches growing toward the center of the tree. Then, if necessary, you can prune selectively along the main limbs, leaving a natural-looking, broad, and bushy top.*

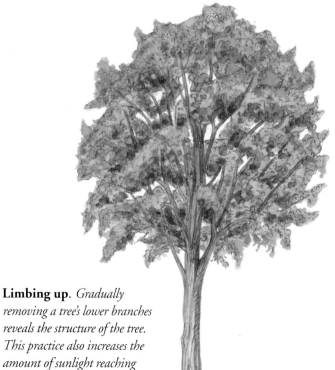

Limbing up. *Gradually removing a tree's lower branches reveals the structure of the tree. This practice also increases the amount of sunlight reaching the ground, making it easier to grow grass and flowers around the tree. Limbing up also gives more headroom beneath the tree's canopy. As a general rule, don't limb up more than half of the tree's height—less is better. And think twice before limbing up a conifer, because it could ruin its natural shape.*

Stop! Don't Top.

Topping—reducing the height of a mature tree by lopping off the top limbs of its canopy—is the quickest way to ruin a tree. What's more, it doesn't reduce the height of a tree for long. Unlike a bushy hedge that soon sprouts new growth after being sheared, a mature tree won't grow back in a natural-looking way when trunk leaders or top branches are pruned to stubs. Instead, the tree sends out scores of weak shoots from the cutoff points; often these shoots are taller, coarser, and denser than the natural top would be. Moreover, topped trees often develop heart rot, eventually re-sulting in hollow trunks that are susceptible to breakage during storms.

Some topped trees may eventually regain much of their original beauty, but the recovery can take decades. A good professional arborist will not top a tree but instead will try other techniques to scale back the tree's size.

Choosing the Right Tree

When it comes to choosing trees for planting in smaller gardens and patios or for adorning a lawn, not just any tree will do. Size, shape, canopy density, and root habits all demand consideration.

In small gardens—as well as in courtyards, on patios and terraces, and near decks—you want a well-mannered, smaller tree that won't drop messy fruits or seeds, whose foliage doesn't harbor insects, and whose root systems won't pry up pavement or damage foundations. Smaller deciduous trees offer the most abundant choices. They require maintenance chiefly in autumn, when you'll have to sweep up the fallen leaves. A classic Southern favorite is crepe myrtle, offering quick shade, showy summer flowers, colorful fall foliage, and handsome winter bark. If you prefer the year-round foliage of an evergreen tree, consider planting 'Little Gem' Southern magnolia, a small-growing selection of the South's signature native tree. Many palms, especially in Florida, serve admirably as patio accent trees (see pages 138–139). Some small trees grow quickly—crepe myrtle and glossy privet, for example—while others, including Japanese maple and sourwood, take their sweet time gaining size. If you choose one of the slower-growing kinds, consider planting a fairly mature specimen.

A good lawn tree should cast some shade yet let enough light through its canopy so that grass will grow well beneath it. Whether you choose a large- or small-growing tree depends on the size of the lawn and the relative dominance you want the tree to assume. In an open stretch of lawn, a larger tree can bring needed balance to the landscape. Strategically placed in a front-yard lawn, a tree can frame the view of your house. Avoid trees that cast dense shade, have low-growing branches or surface roots, or drop a lot of litter. Unfortunately, some of the South's favorite trees have one or more of those traits. Beech, ginkgo (female trees), hemlock, pin oak, Southern magnolia, and sweet gum spell trouble when planted in a lawn; all are better underplanted with shade-loving ground covers or shrubs.

The list at right highlights the South's best bets.

With deep roots and few pests, sourwood (Oxydendrum arboreum) *is one of the best trees for planting close to a house, patio, or deck. Dependable fall foliage color is another asset.*

FOR SMALL SPACES

Amur maple *Acer tataricum ginnala*
Crepe myrtle *Lagerstroemia indica*
Drake Chinese elm *Ulmus parvifolia 'Drake'*
Eastern redbud *Cercis canadensis*
Flowering dogwood *Cornus florida*
Fragrant snowbell *Styrax obassia*
Glossy privet* *Ligustrum lucidum*
Goldenrain tree *Koelreuteria paniculata*
Japanese maple *Acer palmatum*
Korean stewartia *Stewartia koreana*
Lilac chaste tree *Vitex agnus-castus*
Little Gem Southern magnolia*
  Magnolia grandiflora 'Little Gem'
Orchid tree *Bauhinia*
PALMS* (some small types)
Persian parrotia *Parrotia persica*
Serviceberry *Amelanchier*
Sourwood *Oxydendrum arboreum*
Sweet bay *Magnolia virginiana*
Sweet olive* *Osmanthus fragrans*
Texas mountain laurel* *Sophora secundiflora*

FOR LAWNS

Chinese elm *Ulmus parvifolia*
Chinese pistache *Pistacia chinensis*
Crepe myrtle *Lagerstroemia indica*
Fringe tree *Chionanthus virginicus*
Japanese zelkova *Zelkova serrata*
Live oak* *Quercus virginiana*
Loblolly pine* *Pinus taeda*
PALMS*
Red maple *Acer rubrum*
Red oak *Quercus rubra*
River birch *Betula nigra*
Scarlet oak *Quercus coccinea*
Shortleaf pine* *Pinus echinata*
Thornless honey locust *Gleditsia triacanthos inermis*

*Evergreen

Palms

Despite their association with perpetually warm climates, many palms are surprisingly cold hardy. Windmill palm, one of the hardiest, tolerates lows of 5°F. Many others can withstand brief periods of freezing temperatures, making them suitable even for milder areas of the Lower South.

Wherever palms are planted, they create striking focal points. Use them to line a long driveway or the perimeter of a landscape, shade a deck, serve as solo accents, or create an evergreen backdrop. Some, such as Mediterranean fan palm and lady palm, remain shrublike for many years—thriving under taller trees, in mixed borders, and in entryway and courtyard plantings.

Palms and swimming pools are a natural combination. They look absolutely "right" together—and the palms don't continually shed leaves into the water or buckle paving with their roots. Palm fronds reflect beautifully in the pool's mirrored surface, as do the sculptural trunks. Night lighting produces especially dramatic effects. You can backlight palms to cast dramatic shadows, shine spotlights up from ground level to highlight majestic forms, or direct lights to showcase them as dark silhouettes on a pale wall.

The world of palms contains countless kinds, similar in general characteristics but different in details. The modest assortment presented here represents time-tested types well suited to the South.

BAMBOO PALM *(Chamaedorea).* Several species, most with clumping, bamboolike growth. All grow slowly to 5–10 ft. Need shade and ample water. Frost tender.

CABBAGE PALM *(Sabal palmetto).* Single-trunked palm, slow growing to 90 ft. Dense, globular head is formed by fanlike leaves 5–8 ft. across. Tolerates wind, salt spray, and sand. Hardy to 20°F.

CANARY ISLAND DATE PALM *(Phoenix canariensis).* Big, heavy-trunked plant to 60 ft. tall; gracefully arching, featherlike fronds can form a crown up to 50 ft. wide. Young plants do well in pots. Hardy to 20°F.

Slow-growing Mediterranean fan palm serves as a large shrub, making a dramatic statement in the landscape.

CHINESE FAN PALM *(Livistona chinensis).* Fanlike, dark green fronds are divided into numerous segments that droop attractively at their tips. Plant remains trunkless for years; in time it can reach 15 ft. tall, with a broad crown. Makes a fine patio palm if sheltered from wind and hot afternoon sun. Hardy to 22°F.

LADY PALM *(Rhapis).* Slender, bamboolike stems bear glossy, dark green leaves in fanlike formation. Plants grow slowly, make good screen plants. *R. excelsa* grows 5–12 ft. *R. humilis* reaches 18 ft. All prefer rich, moist soil, protection from sun and wind. Hardy to 22°F.

MEDITERRANEAN FAN PALM *(Chamaerops humilis).* Spiny leafstalks terminate in fans of green to bluish green. Natural habit is clumping, but you can limit it to just a single trunk. Either way, growth is slow—to

Cabbage palm   Senegal date palm

20 ft. high and, in clump form, to about 20 ft. wide. Plants endure baking sun, are hardy to 6°F.

PINDO PALM *(Butia capitata)*. Slow-growing palm features feathery, arching, gray-green fronds on a heavy trunk attractively patterned in time with stubs of old fronds. Eventual height is 10–20 ft.; red, edible fruits are decorative in summer. Hardy to 15°F.

PYGMY DATE PALM *(Phoenix roebelinii)*. Fine-textured fronds are featherlike and gracefully arching on an upright trunk; grows slowly to 6–10 ft. high. Wind-resistant but hardy only to 26°F. Silver date palm *(P. sylvestris)* is similar but taller (to 30 ft.), with gray-green fronds; plant is hardy to 22°F.

QUEEN PALM *(Syagrus romanzoffiana)*. Plumelike fronds to 15 ft. spring from atop a fast-growing trunk eventually 30–50 ft. tall. Needs abundant water, regular fertilizing, and shelter from strong winds. Reliably hardy to 25°F (but with leaf damage).

SENEGAL DATE PALM *(Phoenix reclinata)*. Picturesque clumps consist of multiple curving trunks to 20–30 ft., though you can limit plant to a single-trunked tree of about the same height with a fountainlike crown to 20 ft. across. Plant is damaged at 25°F, but will survive temperatures a bit lower.

WINDMILL PALM *(Trachycarpus fortunei)*. Stiff, upright palm can reach 30 ft. in warmer parts of its adapted range. Trunk is covered in hairlike fibers which make it appear thicker at its top. Compact crown consists of 3-ft.-wide fanlike fronds. Appearance is better with shelter from wind. Hardy to 5°F.

Chinese fan palm

Mediterranean fan palm

Pindo palm

Queen palm   Lady palm   Windmill palm   Bamboo palm   Pygmy date palm   Canary Island date palm

Shrubs

Except for a few specialty flowering sorts—roses, azaleas, and rhododendrons, for example—shrubs are the garden's equivalent of Rodney Dangerfield: they get no respect. This is quite unfair, as shrubs are responsible for establishing a landscape's framework. They're the stable plantings that influence views, direct circulation, and make a smooth transition from tree canopy to ground level. You can use the larger ones to punctuate the landscape in a less dominant manner than trees; and, of course, shrubs have a traditional use as foundation plantings (see page 142)—even when there's no real foundation to mask. As tall screens and hedges, they provide privacy, block unpleasant sights and sounds, and keep away unwelcome visitors. The shelter they make can create microclimates that allow

survival of more tender plants that might otherwise succumb to cold in exposed locations.

That's not to suggest that shrubs are purely utilitarian workhorses. Shrub choice and use define a garden's style. Closely clipped hedges lend formality; shrubs with arching branches impart a carefree grace; and, of course, the myriad flowering shrubs bring life to the garden and form the basis for its overall color palette. Judiciously placed, just a single flowering shrub can become the garden's star, drawing all attention to its moment of splendor.

Like trees, shrubs are either evergreen or deciduous. Evergreen types are traditional Southern favorites, giving the garden year-round form and substance. And evergreens also make effective backdrops for plants

FACING PAGE *Given the light afternoon shade it prefers, bigleaf hydrangea* (Hydrangea macrophylla) *forms a symmetrical mound, sporting handsome foliage and heads of showy late-spring and summer flowers.*

with showy flowers and foliage. Many deciduous shrubs, on the other hand, embody a looseness and grace that evergreen types may lack—and they often compensate for their winter bareness with colorful seasonal displays of flowers, fruits, or foliage.

Pruning Shrubs

Nearly all shrubs need some pruning, whether regular or occasional, to maintain their form and, in some cases, their vigor. It helps to know in advance of purchase what sort of pruning a shrub will need.

Natural size is a vital point to consider when you make your selection. Be very sure to match a shrub's potential size to the place it will occupy in your garden. A shrub you constantly have to cut back in order to free a doorway or keep a walkway clear is the wrong choice for the location. In the same vein, make sure that shrubs located in the flower border won't quickly overwhelm the space. In both situations, the necessary restrictive pruning will compromise the plant's inherent beauty.

Best pruning times depend on the type or behavior of the shrub. Prune spring-flowering shrubs just after their flowers fade and before new growth initiates. Summer-flowering shrubs should be pruned in late winter or early spring; their new growth then will bear the summer blooms. You can prune nonflowering evergreens at almost any time of year.

Proper Parterres

Distinctive components of formal, historic, and herb gardens, parterres traditionally consist of garden spaces defined by rows of neatly clipped, low-growing shrubs. Because of their precise, symmetrical layouts, they're particularly effective when viewed from above—as from a second-story window or balcony. Whether used as a formal entryway statement or as an organized showpiece in an herb or vegetable garden, a parterre has but one requirement—that it be neatly maintained.

The most recognizable form of parterre is the "knot garden," where clipped shrubs create intricate geometric patterns. Shrubs used to form the knot should be evergreen types that tolerate regular pruning or shearing. The two most common choices are edging boxwood (*Buxus sempervirens* 'Suffruticosa') and germander (*Teucrium chamaedrys*). To add color to a knot garden parterre, you can incorporate any of several shrubs with non-green foliage. Red-leafed 'Crimson Pygmy' Japanese barberry (*Berberis thunbergii* 'Crimson Pygmy'), gray-leafed English lavender (*Lavandula angustifolia*), and silvery gray lavender cotton (*Santolina chamaecyparissus*) all take well to the necessary frequent clipping. Hard pruning during the hot summer months can cause dieback, so lightly shear these shrubs often during the year.

Once the shrubs have established the outlines of your parterre, you can fill in its interior spaces. Seasonal annuals and bulbs are natural choices, but you might also try low-growing vegetables with attractive leaves (such as purple-leafed cabbages or bright green lettuces), herbs, perennials, and ground covers.

A focal point in a parterre will make the composition come alive. The parterre's center, for example, can be just the spot for a choice urn, a fountain, a sundial, a gazing ball, or a piece of classic statuary.

Foundation Plantings

Garden designers may dismiss the idea of "foundation planting" as outmoded and cliché, but to many home gardeners, the planting of shrubs at the base of the house still is an essential part of a landscape. Some sort of planting, after all, is usually needed to make a pleasing transition from house to lawn or garden.

The history of foundation planting starts in past times when homes were built on high foundations, the first floor reached by a set of steps. To mask or soften the exposed foundation, large, bulky shrubs would be planted along the house's perimeter. Over time, home styles changed and foundations lowered—but homeowners still planted the time-honored foundation-plant shrubs. The resulting wall of shrubbery needed constant cutting back to prevent windows from vanishing and the house from drowning in a sea of foliage. Thus, "foundation planting" got a bad rap—not because of flawed concept but due to simply poor choice of plants for contemporary architecture.

Even though today's homeowners confront a variety of architectural styles, the concept of foundation planting is still valid. These plants can visually anchor the house to the site, hide utility hardware and downspouts, and direct people to the main entry. But for foundation plantings to serve your house well, you should keep the following guidelines in mind.

∾ Pay close attention to size. A shrub needing constant cutting back is the wrong choice for that location; choose plants that will grow no taller than you need. Also check the spread of the plants and space them to allow for normal growth; too-close spacing fills in quickly but can lead to disease and pruning issues later.

∾ Keep it simple. A planting of three to four different plants presents a unified appearance, while a patchwork assortment of different shrubs just looks disorganized.

∾ If your house facade is beautiful, show it off. Don't hide it behind a mass of foliage; plant ground covers instead.

∾ Coordinate the style of planting to the style of your house. A traditional, symmetrical house, for example, looks best with a simple, symmetrical planting.

∾ De-emphasize the negative. If you plant tall, narrow evergreens at the corners of a tall, narrow house, you only highlight the home's vertical thrust, making it appear perched on the land. Instead, plant rounded or spreading shrubs to anchor the house to a seemingly broader platform and make it seem wider.

∾ Choose colors carefully. If you select flowering shrubs for foundation planting, be sure their flowers won't clash with the house colors or be so similar that they simply fade into the architecture.

Closely manicured shrubs form a stairstep foundation screen, gently linking this vintage Craftsman bungalow to ground level.

LEFT *A mass planting of 'Flower Carpet' roses wraps around this foundation without blocking the view from the full-length windows.*

FOR OPEN VIEWS

Listed here are some attractive, generally slow-growing shrubs you can plant beneath windows without fear of losing the view. Heights listed are for mature plants.

Azalea *Rhododendron*, 1–5 ft.
Andorra juniper *Juniperus horizontalis* 'Plumosa', 1½ ft.
Common gardenia *Gardenia jasminoides* 'Radicans', 1 ft.
Dwarf camellia *Camellia hiemalis*, 2 ft.
Dwarf Chinese holly *Ilex cornuta* 'Rotunda', 3–4 ft.
Dwarf Japanese pittosporum *Pittosporum tobira* 'Wheeler's Dwarf', 3–4 ft.
Dwarf nandina *Nandina domestica* 'Harbor Dwarf', 1½–2 ft.
Dwarf yaupon *Ilex vomitoria* 'Nana', 1–2 ft.
Edging boxwood *Buxus sempervirens* 'Suffruticosa', 2–3 ft.
Glossy abelia *Abelia* × *grandiflora* 'Francis Mason', 3–4 ft.
Himalayan sweet box *Sarcococca hookeriana humilis*, 1½ ft.
Indian hawthorn *Rhaphiolepis indica* 'Ballerina', 2 ft.
Japanese barberry *Berberis thunbergii* 'Crimson Pygmy', 1½ ft.
Japanese holly *Ilex crenata* 'Helleri', 1–2 ft.
Shrub rose *Rosa* 'Flower Carpet', 1–2 ft.
Spreading English yew *Taxus baccata* 'Repandens', 2–4 ft.
Texas ranger *Leucophyllum frutescens* 'Compactum', 3–4 ft.

ABOVE *A Southern favorite for foundation plantings, azaleas come in many sizes and colors. Bloom time varies from winter through spring.*

Screens and Hedges

Many homeowners face the dilemma of maintaining the openness of their landscape while preserving their privacy. How do you see out without others seeing in? One solution for screening and privacy is to build a fence or wall (see pages 86–89, 122–123). But this can entail considerable initial expense—not to mention maintenance and future repairs. A simpler solution lies in strategic planting of shrubs to block just enough reciprocal vision to give you privacy while maintaining a view. Planted screens do take a few years to fill in completely, but they generally cost far less than constructed screens and create a far softer, more natural appearance.

Shrub screens can be either formal or informal. Sheared hedges represent the formal approach—neat and tidy, for sure, but a type of planting that demands frequent maintenance to retain its flat, wall-like surface. Formal hedges of privet or boxwood are common throughout the South, but you can assume each one gets sheared at least four times every year.

ABOVE *A single row of limbed-up crepe myrtles* (Lagerstroemia indica) *effectively separates the driveways between two homes.*

RIGHT *Heavenly bamboo* (Nandina domestica), *with strongly vertical stems, makes a handsome evergreen hedge or screen in narrow spaces.*

For practical reasons, most gardeners opt for informal screens—shrubs planted inline, as hedging plants are, but left to grow naturally with just the occasional light pruning to control size or head back wildly errant growth. Evergreen shrubs will provide screening throughout the year. Good candidates for informal evergreen screens in the South include glossy abelia *(Abelia × grandiflora)*, Carolina cherry laurel *(Prunus caroliniana)*, Florida leucothoe *(Agarista populifolia)*, holly *(Ilex)*, Japanese pittosporum *(Pittosporum tobira)*, nandina or heavenly bamboo *(Nandina domestica)*, oleander *(Nerium oleander)*, and Texas ranger *(Leucophyllum frutescens)*.

A number of deciduous shrubs also form good screens during their leafy part of the year. Among the best of these are doublefile viburnum *(Viburnum plicatum tomentosum),* forsythia, and winter honeysuckle *(Lonicera fragrantissima);* even in winter, these will partially block a view with their thick network of bare branches.

Privacy is but one reason to plant shrubs as screens. You can use them as living walls to segment a landscape into separate garden "rooms." By carefully locating screening shrubs, you can create mysteries and reveal surprises as the plants direct traffic to areas hidden behind or around them. Or you simply may want to locate shrubs to focus your view on a vista or to serve as a backdrop for a special focal point such as a garden sculpture.

From Shrub to Tree

Everyone knows what a tree is: something big, with one to several trunks topped by a canopy of foliage. You can walk under it, or lie in its shade. A shrub, then, is anything smaller with leaves right to the ground: you walk *around* it. Well...yes and no. Some familiar shrubs need only a gardener's nudge to become small trees—maybe not tall enough to shade a house, but definitely a head of foliage carried on stilts. All you need to do is remove lower branches from a shrub's main stem (or stems) to create a treelike foliage canopy. Some shrubs have few enough main stems that you need only limb them up; with many-stemmed shrubs, you'll also have to thin out the stems, leaving just a few of the strongest to serve as trunks (see page 136).

Why bother to do this? One reason is to salvage a shrub that has become too bulky—*as a shrub*—for its location. By converting it into a small tree, you turn it into something more sculptural and at the same time reduce its overall mass. If the offending bulky shrub impinges on a walkway, for example, this sort of pruning can immediately restore access without sacrificing the plant.

Another reason for performing a shrub-to-tree conversion is simply to open up the landscape. A dense top-to-bottom shrub screen can, in time, become oppressive; but by opening up its lower reaches, you can achieve a sort of hedge on poles which still will retain its screening function.

Shrubs trained to a single trunk are referred to as standards. These range from the quite familiar "tree rose" to large crepe myrtles and hollies used in the landscape as small trees. Some standards are trained specifically for displaying in pots; these include camellias, Chinese hibiscus, Indian hawthorn, some junipers, lantana, and princess flower.

With all standards and limbed-up shrubs, regularly remove all sprouts that form on the bare stems; otherwise, plants will eventually return to their natural shrubby form.

TOP *Usually grown as a dense, twiggy shrub, winged euonymus* (Euonymus alatus) *can be pruned into an especially graceful small tree.*

ABOVE *Oleander* (Nerium oleander), *familiar as a shrub in milder parts of the South, makes an eye-catching small flowering tree.*

Roses

Roses have always had a special place in the hearts of Southern gardeners—and no wonder. They offer beauty, fragrance, diversity, and general ease of culture. True, foliage diseases can be a thorny problem with some roses, particularly in the South's most humid climates. But now more than ever before gardeners have access to a broad array of modern lovelies developed for beauty, toughness, and easy care, as well as a growing number of heirloom favorites that always have been sound landscape performers.

In specialty catalogs, you'll find roses listed according to class: hybrid tea, shrub, floribunda, climber, hybrid musk, and so on. With few exceptions, class makes little difference: just choose according to what size and shape of plant you need; from calf-high miniatures to house-high climbers, you can find a rose for just about any sunny garden niche. But if you're looking for long-stemmed beauties for cutting, turn to the hybrid tea class where you'll find large, shapely blooms in the full range of rose colors and patterns.

TOP *Dark pink 'Old Blush', pale pink 'Ballerina', and climbing* Rosa multiflora carnea *combine in a floriferous welcome to the garden beyond.*

MIDDLE *A garden bench is engulfed in scented blooms of 'Constance Spry'—a modern rose embodying the voluptuous charm of 19th-century favorites.*

BOTTOM *From spring through summer and on into fall, 'Ballerina' bears clusters of sculpturally perfect single flowers on a rounded, densely foliaged shrub.*

Landscaping with Roses

Roses are, by and large, vigorous plants that need only sun (at least half a day), water, and a bit of fertilizer to thrive. But do pay attention to a variety's ultimate height and spread. Roses grow best when they have room to develop, and routine maintenance is easier when plants aren't crowded. As long as you meet these simple requirements, your roses will shine in a number of roles.

Used as flowering shrubs, roses make valuable contributions to mixed plantings of perennials, annuals, and other shrubs. You can use the more vigorous hybrid teas for a supply of vase-quality flowers—but the most prized types for mixed plantings are shrub roses, climbers, miniatures, and heirloom varieties. By including both the spring bloomers and the repeat-flowering types, you can achieve great variety in flower, foliage, and plant styles over a long season. Some roses even produce colorful fruits ("hips") to enliven the autumn scene.

Mass plantings of a single variety offer another display option. Shrub types and some of the heirloom sorts make excellent informal hedges of various heights. Larger kinds serve as background and barrier plants; lower-growing types can define spaces within a garden. To border a pathway with color from spring until autumn, look no further than the miniature roses.

Roses also shine as solo performers. A single shrub rose beside a gate or entryway presents a colorful welcome. Just one climbing rose can transform an arch, pergola, or rail fence from stark utility to a flowery focal point—or become an unexpected adornment to a tall-growing tree. And a judiciously sited standard ("tree") rose immediately becomes a garden star.

Of course, there is always the traditional rose bed in which you can showcase mixed-variety plantings of hybrid teas and grandifloras. This is the most efficient setup for a cutting garden and will accommodate the most roses in a given area. Formal planting arrangements are typical—roses set out in rows of military precision, each bed separated from the next by pathways of lawn or paving. To introduce some informality, you can lay out the beds in flowing curves to create irregular shapes.

ABOVE *'Dortmund' shows off white-centered red blossoms against a backdrop of highly glossy foliage. The prickly canes discourage predators from ambushing the birdhouse, while a lavish crop of hips offers winter forage.*

BELOW *Fragrant butter yellow to gold blossoms endear 'Graham Thomas' to legions of gardeners. It's a modest climber in mild-winter regions, a slender shrub where winters are colder.*

Choosing the Right Rose

Shopping for roses is a delightful experience, but the sheer number of varieties available can make choosing difficult. The lists that follow include a selection of proven Southern performers, grouped according to characteristics and common garden uses. Nowadays, most gardeners expect roses to flower from spring to frost—exceptions being some of the spring-only heirloom varieties. Nearly all the roses listed here will bloom repeatedly until cold weather shuts them down. These lists are ordered by color: from white through shades of yellow, orange, pink, red, and purple.

Small hedges, borders, containers. Little roses that bloom constantly will never go out of fashion; they're just too effective in too many settings. They can be used in drifts like perennials, as color accents in containers, as low hedges or borders along a bed, path, or driveway. The following miniatures, polyanthas, and floribundas all form bushy plants 1½–3 ft. high: white 'Katharina Zeimet' and 'White Pet', white-and-green 'Green Ice', white-and-pink 'Magic Carrousel' and

'Sweet Vivien', yellow 'Fairhope' and 'Rise 'n' Shine', yellow-and-red 'Rainbow's End', pale apricot 'Grüss an Aachen' and 'Jean Kenneally', orange 'Impatient' and 'Pride 'n' Joy', coral 'Margo Koster' and 'Millie Walters', pink 'China Doll' and 'Pinkie', scarlet 'Show Biz', red 'Beauty Secret' and 'Martha Gonzales', and mauve 'Baby Faurax' and 'Sweet Chariot'.

Medium hedges, borders, specimens. These bushy plants grow 4–5 ft. tall and wide: white 'Iceberg', apricot 'Perle d'Or', pink-and-white 'Ballerina' and 'La Marne', pale pink 'Bonica', pink 'Belinda's Dream', 'Carefree Wonder', and 'The Fairy', pink-and-red 'Archduke Charles', and red 'Europeana' and 'Valentine'.

Tall hedges, borders, specimens. These big bushes grow 6 ft. tall and wide or larger: yellow 'Graham Thomas', pale peach 'Sally Holmes', orange 'Westerland', light salmon pink 'Sparrieshoop', salmon pink 'Queen Elizabeth', pale pink 'Heritage', red 'Linda Campbell', soft crimson 'Mrs. B.R. Cant', mauve 'Hansa', and multicolored 'Mutabilis'.

Ground covers. Some roses sprawl on the ground or form low, graceful mounds. They cover banks, cascade over walls, or fill large containers. The excellent 'Flower

TOP LEFT *'Sun Flare'*
TOP CENTER *'Sombreuil'*
TOP RIGHT *'Mutabilis'*
BOTTOM LEFT *'Margo Koster'*
BOTTOM CENTER *'Europeana'*

Carpet' roses are available in white, apple blossom (light pink), pink, coral, and red. Also try white 'Alba Meidiland', 'Nozomi', and 'Sea Foam', pale pink 'Pearl Drift', red-and-yellow 'Ralph's Creeper', red 'Red Cascade', and mauve 'Magic Carpet'.

Superfragrants. Distinctively scented roses are a double delight. Plant them where you can enjoy the beauty and perfume close-up. Good choices include white 'Fair Bianca' and 'Kronprincessin Viktoria', yellow 'Sun Flare', peach 'Ambridge Rose' and 'Belle Story', apricot 'Mrs. Oakley Fisher', orange 'Fragrant Cloud', pale pink 'Souvenir de la Malmaison', creamy pink 'Clotilde Soupert', silvery pink 'La France', light pink 'Hermosa', dark pink 'Basye's Blueberry', 'Madame Isaac Pereire', and 'Rose de Rescht', dark red 'Oklahoma', red-and-white 'Double Delight', and lavender 'Angel Face'.

Short climbers for pillars. These restrained growers reach 8–10 ft. tall: white 'Prosperity', yellow 'Golden Showers', apricot pink 'Abraham Darby', pink 'Aloha', dark pink 'Madame Isaac Pereire', dark red 'Don Juan', and soft crimson 'Maggie'.

Medium-size climbers for fences, trellises. These roses climb to 10–12 ft.: white 'Sombreuil', yellow 'Yellow Blaze', peach 'Compassion', apricot 'Buff

Beauty', pink 'Parade', red 'Red Fountain', and lavender 'Climbing Angel Face'.

Large, vigorous climbers for arbors, walls. Great roses that grow 12–20 ft. tall include white 'Climbing Iceberg', cream 'Madame Alfred Carrière', yellow 'Mermaid', salmon pink 'Climbing Queen Elizabeth', pale pink 'Climbing Cécile Brunner' and 'New Dawn', rich pink 'Constance Spry', and red 'Climbing Crimson Glory' and 'Dortmund'.

Thornless roses. Climbers include white 'Aimée Vibert', white or yellow *Rosa banksiae* (known as Lady Banks' rose), apricot 'Crépuscule', pink 'Climbing Pinkie', and deep pink 'Zéphirine Drouhin'. 'Veilchenblau' is a purple rambler. Bushes include white 'Marie Pavié', yellow-and-pink 'Mrs. Dudley Cross', light pink 'Heritage', cerise pink 'Paul Neyron', red 'Smooth Prince', and purple 'Reine des Violettes'.

Roses that bloom in light shade. Among climbers, look for pale pink 'Climbing Cécile Brunner' and lavender-pink 'Lavender Lassie'. Bushes include white 'Marie Pavié', pale apricot 'Penelope', and red 'Eutin'. Pink 'Old Blush' may be grown as a bush or a climber.

TOP LEFT *'Fragrant Cloud'*
TOP CENTER *'Graham Thomas'*
TOP RIGHT *'Bonica'*
BOTTOM LEFT *'Sea Foam'*
BOTTOM CENTER *'Rainbow's End'*

trees compete with grass roots for moisture and nutrients. In these challenging situations, a shade-loving ground cover will give you more satisfaction than lawn grass. If you are trying to garden on sloping ground, the degree of slope determines whether or not you can plant a lawn. Grass does a fine job of stabilizing gentle slopes to prevent erosion, but steep slopes are hazardous to mow. The cutoff point at which a slope is too steep to mow is about a 30 percent grade—a slope that rises 3 feet for every 10 feet of distance. If you have a grade greater than 30 percent, plant the slope with ground cover or consider terracing it with a series of retaining walls.

After you've determined your garden's best lawn site, think about how you'll want to use the lawn. If you have children, you may want a grassy space large enough to serve as a play area. If, on the other hand, you simply want some green as contrast to other garden plants, a small lawn may be just right. In any landscape, determine where regular foot traffic will occur, then install permanent walkways or pavers so the lawn won't be marred by a scruffy dirt trail.

In planning a lawn, always consider maintenance. For best appearance and health, a lawn needs weekly mowing during much of the growing season, periodic fertilizing, watering during dry spells, and, perhaps, pest and disease control. If trees are nearby, raking will be a routine chore. How much time you're willing to devote to lawn care should influence the size of lawn you plant.

Deciding on Shape

Just as lawn sizes vary, so do the shapes they take. What shape you choose—rectangular or square, circular or oval, angular, or free-form—will depend on garden topography, existing plants and beds, architectural

Lawns

Throughout the South, you'll find one feature common to nearly all homes: a lawn. While this may sound simply like tradition, a manicured lawn also has aesthetic and practical value. Consider, for example, that a lawn offers the perfect spot for outdoor social gatherings, a convenient field for impromptu sports or children's play, and, of course, the perfect vantage point from which to savor the beauty of the surrounding garden. No wonder so many Southern homeowners think of the lawn as a garden's foundation.

You'll find the best lawns growing in relatively level, sunny areas where grass has the soil all to itself. Too much shade, especially beneath low-branching trees, practically defeats lawn growth, and shallow-rooted style, and personal preference. Even regional geography can play a part. The flat lands of the Coastal South in cities like New Orleans and Charleston, for example, favor formal design; gardens in rolling, interior regions, such as Birmingham, often feature larger lawns in sweeping, curvilinear shapes.

Perhaps the most common lawn treatment seen in new suburban developments is the mega-lawn: each homeowner's front yard flows seamlessly into the next, forming a neighborhood lawn-without-boundaries. While efficient to mow—you just whiz back and forth between property lines—it represents a missed design opportunity. By defining a lawn's shape with a surround of trees, shrubs, and ground covers, you can achieve a landscape setting for your home and a more inviting space for outdoor living.

Whatever shape you choose for a lawn, the line its edge creates will have the greatest visual impact. If this line isn't pleasing, you won't be happy with the design. Establishing gracefully curving lines can be particularly challenging; you want smooth, sweeping curves rather than overly wiggly, wavy edges. An easy way to test out and establish a curving line is to use garden hoses to plot the curves. Lay the hoses on the ground where you think you want the lawn margin, then adjust them until you get a line you like. When you're satisfied, mark the boundary with landscape marking paint.

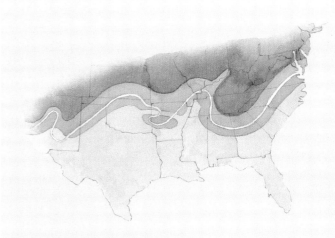

Grasses for the South

Southern lawn grasses separate into two groups—warm-season types (Bahia, Bermuda, St. Augustine, buffalo, carpet, and centipede grasses as well as zoysia) and cool-season grasses (Kentucky bluegrass, perennial ryegrass, and tall fescue). Warm-season grasses thrive when daytime highs rise above 90°F and night temperatures remain above 70°F. Freezing weather turns them brown and may even kill some kinds. Cool-season grasses are at their best when daytime temperatures are in the 70s and 80s and night temperatures are 10 to 20°F cooler; periods of hot, dry weather greatly stress them. Unlike the warm-season types, these grasses remain green over winter.

Use the map above as a general guide to selecting the best grass type for your region. The distinct white line divides the South into the southern warm- and northern cool-season regions; the shaded areas on either side of the white line indicate transition zones where warm-season grasses may be grown in sunny, protected locations and cool-season types will grow in shady spots at higher elevations or with frequent watering. The best transitional grasses are Bermuda grass, Kentucky bluegrass, perennial ryegrass, tall fescue, zoysia, and buffalo grass.

The map is a good general guide, but local microclimates may vary conditions significantly. For good specific advice on successful lawn grasses, consult your Cooperative Extension office or an established local nursery. Or ask neighbors who have particularly attractive lawns.

Minimize Lawn Maintenance

All lawns require frequent attention, but these tips can help reduce the amount of time you have to spend caring for your lawn.

∽ Install a sprinkler system—ideally before you put in the lawn. Moving hoses around to water a lawn is time-consuming.

∽ Choose a grass well suited to your climate and to the sort of wear and tear it will get. By making the right selection, you'll reduce the time needed to combat insects and diseases and to repair damage from use.

∽ Reduce the number of sharp corners in your lawn. You waste time and energy maneuvering the mower in and out of tight spaces.

∽ Keep obstructions (birdhouses, lamp posts, mailboxes) out of the lawn. Having to mow and trim around them adds to maintenance time.

∽ Install a mowing strip between the lawn and planting beds. A ribbon of brick, stone, or concrete just wide enough to accommodate the mower's wheels will let you neatly trim the lawn's edge. It also prevents the lawn from traveling into planting beds.

∽ During dry summer weather, mow the grass a bit higher than normal. You won't have to water it as frequently to keep it green.

∽ If you have groups of small trees in the lawn, plant ground cover in drifts to fill in between the trees. Then you'll only need to mow around the ground cover rather than between and around individual trees.

LEFT AND INSET *A small zoysia lawn forms a greenbelt between brick patio and flower bed. A brick mowing strip at the bed's edge facilitates mowing and keeps the lawn's edge in place.*

ABOVE RIGHT *A green river of tall fescue flows between house and neighboring woodland. Mulched ground on either side of the lawn clearly delineates the boundaries.*

RIGHT *A closely cropped circular lawn makes a verdant "landing pad" transition zone between different levels in this hillside garden.*

Winter Lawns

Whether you have a warm-season grass or a cool-season one, you can enjoy your lawn's appearance in winter. Warm-season grasses (see page 151) turn to shades of tan as cold weather arrives. Rather than bemoan their lack of winter green, you can capitalize on this color change by bordering the lawn with an evergreen ground cover to highlight the beige outdoor "carpet." In contrast, cool-season grasses (also on page 151) remain green in cold weather. A cool-season green lawn surrounded by the bare silhouettes of deciduous trees and shrubs becomes a verdant showpiece in the prevailing winter gray.

Lawn Alternatives

Lawn grass may be the country's best-loved ground cover, but it's not the only act in town. In fact, it may *not* be the best choice for your garden. If you have no need for a lawn, if your property doesn't have a good spot for grass, or if you simply don't want to put in the maintenance time a good lawn requires, then you should check out alternative ground covers.

When you look beyond lawn, you'll discover that other ground covers present countless opportunities not offered by grasses. Some grow easily in shade and even with competition from tree roots; some thrive on slopes too steep for a lawn; many prosper with far less water than a lawn demands—and without the need for mowing. Ground covers also invite imaginative combinations of textures and colors. Some offer showy flowers, while others boast colored or variegated foliage. You'll find ground covers that truly hug the soil and others that form uniform to undulating surfaces up to 3 feet high. Lovely tapestry plantings can be crafted from different kinds of ground covers or by using different selections of one kind. Of course, ground covers also can be purely utilitarian—suppressing weeds and dust, preventing erosion on slopes—and the lowest-growing types will give you the flat uniformity of a lawn.

When considering what ground covers to plant, look for ones certain to do well in your climate zone (see map pages 216–217). Just because something is stunning in Asheville doesn't mean that it will give the same performance in Orlando. Also, be sure to consider what you expect of the ground cover. If you need to blanket a large area fairly quickly, the vigorous vining and self-rooting types (such as Algerian and English ivies, and Asian and star jasmines) will satisfy. To cover a slope or bank, look for wide-spreading plants (many low-growing junipers, for example) or semi-vining types like wintercreeper euonymus that root as their stems spread.

Gardeners who have attempted growing a lawn in shade know how hard it is to keep moss from invading their turf. Some have decided to embrace the enemy and deliberately encourage a moss "lawn" by keeping the area moist and removing competing plants. Mosses come in many different shades of green and can form striking soil blankets in light-starved parts of the garden. Best of all, they never need mowing or fertilizing.

The final alternative to lawn is not any kind of plant at all—it's mulch! A bed neatly mulched with bark or pine straw can visually unite a planting of trees, shrubs, or perennials, highlighting flowers and foliage against its neutral tones. As long as you replenish it from time to time, you'll not be bothered with having to pull weeds.

BELOW LEFT *Colorful thymes are a perfect solution for a hard-to-mow slope.*

BELOW *For a no-traffic area, use mondo grass to replicate shaggy turf.*

A GROUND COVER SAMPLER

NAME	LIGHT	ZONES*	COMMENTS[†]
Algerian ivy *Hedera canariensis*	Shade	CS,TS	Spreads quickly, will climb; grows 8–10 in. tall.
Asian star jasmine *Trachelospermum asiaticum*	Sun/shade	LS,CS,TS	Tough; spreads quickly, will climb; grows 10–14 in. tall.
Big blue liriope *Liriope muscari*	Part shade/shade	All	Showy summer flowers in blues and white; variegated forms; grows 12–15 in. tall.
Carpet bugleweed *Ajuga reptans*	Sun/shade	US,MS,LS	Blue spring flowers; green or bronze foliage; grows 2–14 in. tall.
Common periwinkle *Vinca minor*	Shade	All	Blue spring flowers; plant spreads quickly; grows 3–6 in. tall.
Cotoneaster	Sun	US,MS,LS	Deciduous and evergreen kinds; showy red berries; grow 1–3 ft. tall.
English ivy *Hedera helix*	Shade	US,MS,LS,CS	Spreads quickly, will climb; grows 6–10 in. tall.
Japanese ardisia *Ardisia japonica*	Part shade/shade	LS,CS	Glossy, leathery foliage, red berries; grows 6–12 in. tall.
Japanese pachysandra *Pachysandra terminalis*	Shade	US,MS,LS	Needs moist, acid, fertile soil; spreads slowly; grows 8–12 in. tall.
Juniper *Juniperus*	Sun	US,MS,LS,CS	Tolerates drought, poor soil; grows 3 in.–3 ft. tall, depending on type.
Mazus *Mazus reptans*	Sun/part shade	US,MS,LS,CS	Showy spring flowers; likes growing between rocks; reaches 1–2 in. tall.
Mondo grass *Ophiopogon japonicus*	Part shade/shade	MS,LS,CS,TS	Carefree appearance like dark green grass; grows 3–8 in. tall, depending on selection.
Sprenger asparagus *Asparagus densiflorus* 'Sprengeri'	Part shade/shade	CS,TS	Light green fronds, fine texture, red berries; grows 1–3 ft. tall.
Thyme *Thymus*	Sun/part shade	US,MS,LS,CS	Fragrant foliage; good for growing between stepping-stones; reaches 2–12 in. tall, depending on type.
Wedelia *Wedelia trilobata*	Sun/part shade	CS,TS	Showy yellow flowers; often invasive; grows 1–1½ ft. tall.
Wintercreeper euonymus *Euonymus fortunei*	Sun/shade	US,MS,LS,CS	Tough; spreads quickly, will climb; grows 4–8 in. tall.

*Upper South (US), Middle South (MS), Lower South (LS), Coastal South (CS), Tropical South (TS) [†]Evergreen unless noted.

Japanese pachysandra

Asian star jasmine

Common periwinkle

Big blue liriope

Vines

Whether softening a bare structure, weaving through a trellis, cloaking an arbor, or scrambling over a wall, vines lend considerable grace to Southern gardens. Their versatility makes them first-rate decorative accents, drawing the viewer's eye upward with the vertical impact they bring to the garden. Among vines, you'll find great diversity. In growth habit, they range from vigorous, far-reaching types to those restrained enough to grow in containers or even hanging baskets. You even have "sociable" vines, like large-flowered clematis, that will mingle with other vines to create composite floral fabrics. Many of the most beloved vines feature colorful flowers or fruits, but some of the widely planted kinds have gained their popularity from beauty of foliage alone.

Because vines continually extend their territory they need routine maintenance to keep them within the bounds you desire. Large, exuberant types (wisteria is a prime example) can extend into nearby trees and to natural areas; their bulk and weight will easily overwhelm and crush small or insubstantial supports. Vines with aerial rootlets (such as English ivy) that firmly attach to surfaces can damage mortar in brick walls. Avoid planting any vine directly against wooden siding, as the moisture and debris trapped by the plant will cause the wood to decay.

ABOVE LEFT *Nothing softens a bare wall better than a vine. This Chinese wisteria attaches to a subtle trellis, covered each year by a cascade of fragrant amethyst blossoms.*

ABOVE *Creativity and craftsmanship combine to produce an inviting spot for spending time enjoying the flowers, the ensemble softened by an arch covered with climbing roses.*

FACING PAGE *Two varieties of large-flowered clematis gracefully thread through a latticework frame, joined by goldflame honeysuckle (Lonicera × heckrottii) in the upper reaches.*

ABOVE *Tropical allamanda (Allamanda cathartica) flaunts its spectacular blossoms year-round in the South's mildest regions. The vines cover great expanses but do need support.*

SOUTHERN FAVORITES

Flowering Vines

Carolina jessamine *Gelsemium sempervirens*
Clematis
Coral vine *Antigonon leptopus*
Crossvine *Bignonia capreolata*
Honeysuckle *Lonicera*
Jasmine *Jasminum*
Rose *Rosa* (climbing kinds)
Star jasmine *Trachelospermum*
Tropical allamanda *Allamanda cathartica*
Trumpet creeper *Campsis*
Wisteria

Decorative-foliage Vines

Bittersweet* *Celastrus*
Boston ivy *Parthenocissus tricuspidata*
Carolina moonseed* *Cocculus carolinus*
English ivy *Hedera helix*
Grape* *Vitis*
Grape ivy *Cissus rhombifolia*
Hop *Humulus lupulus*
Porcelain berry* *Ampelopsis brevipedunculata*
Virginia creeper *Parthenocissus quinquefolia*
Wintercreeper euonymus *Euonymus fortunei*

* Bear colorful fruits

The Garden Composition

Color sets a garden's mood, form establishes its geometry, and texture provides its touch. Together, they make the garden a sensory experience, defining to us its *feel* from the first moment we see it. By learning a few basics, you can make sure your garden creates the sensation you want.

Designing with Color

Would you like your garden to feel calm and peaceful? Then fill it with the *cool colors*—blues, purples, and greens—shown on the right side of the color wheel. If, on the other hand, you prefer a garden that sizzles with excitement and energy, fill it with the *warm colors*—red, orange, and yellow—on the left side of the wheel. Warm colors are also great for accents and focal points. Against green or another color-quiet background, they combine handsomely with each other. Individually, each pairs well with blue.

Visible from afar, warm colors dominate the garden when viewed up close. Cool colors tend to disappear with distance or in the dim light of evening, making the garden composition look washed out. You can solve this problem without compromising the tranquillity of a cool-color border by adding just a few plants in warm hues to the mix.

To make a bold statement, pair *contrasting colors*—those that lie directly opposite each other on the color wheel. For example, try combining purple and yellow,

TOP *True contrast comes from combining color opposites. Here, bright yellow coreopsis pairs with blue-purple sage in a vivid composition leavened by white.*

ABOVE *Harmonious plantings encompass hues between two primary colors. In this example, red bee balm, orange butterfly weed, and yellow-orange-red blanket flower combine in a warm scheme.*

blue and orange, or red and green. These contrasting colors serve to intensify each other. You can also make a *harmonious* composition by adding a close neighbor of one of the contrasting colors—say, purple and yellow with the latter's neighbor, yellow orange.

If you're a beginner, resist the urge to plant one flower of every color you find at the garden center. Instead, plant masses of single colors that ease into each other. To make designing your garden easier, choose a favorite color or combination of colors as the basic theme, then add other plants with foliage or flowers that are harmonious within that color theme. But remember: there are no rules for garden design that can't be broken. The most important thing is that the combinations you choose please you. Like all other forms of art, the beauty of a garden is in the eye of the beholder.

Moderating Color

White, gray, and silver are garden peacemakers, mellowing the heat of competing warm colors, enlivening the tranquillity of cool colors, and bridging or blending all the colors in the garden. It's hard to have too much white, gray, or silver in any garden. Blue also combines or mixes well with any other color: the rarest color found in plants, it is an asset wherever it is used. Just a few blue blossoms can be an effective buffer between clashing colors such as orange and magenta. Make lavish use of all these garden diplomats to separate colors that often collide, such as pink and yellow.

ABOVE LEFT *Just one plant can create a harmonious color picture. The purple tones (and clean white) of these pansies are in perfect harmony with the green of their foliage.*

ABOVE MIDDLE *In a cool-color show, vivid blue lupine combines with annual phlox in shades of pink and blue-toned red.*

ABOVE *Silvery gray leaves of lamb's ears* (Stachys byzantina) *tone down the sharpness of sulfur yellow cushion spurge* (Euphorbia polychroma).

Garden Greens

Green is the mainstay of the garden, providing a handsome backdrop for any color of flower. Variations in shades of green can also create a dramatic accent.

Dark green. Deep green foliage, whether used as a background or in combination with other plants, adds rich texture and a settled, mature look to the garden. A dark green background also adds a feeling of depth to a planting.

Blue green. Blue-green plants have a calming effect, much like a pool of water, and blend easily with all other plant colors. Against a backdrop of dark green or among warm-colored flowers, they also can serve as focal points.

Yellow green. Yellow-green leaves are handsome as a foil, backdrop, or spotlight. They brighten more sedate colors like deep purple or blue, and add a "sunny" spot in shady gardens. Yellow green is a lively backdrop for marine blue flowers, such as forget-me-nots.

Gray green. Frosty gray-green or silver-green foliage cools down hot colors and highlights cool ones. It's also an attractive accent as the single color of a border. Gray-green foliage takes on a special luminescent quality in the evening, especially in moonlight.

Working with Texture

Texture isn't as readily apparent as color when you first glimpse a garden, but it's just as important. A garden filled with only fine-textured, small-leafed plants would be boring. One filled exclusively with coarse, bold foliage would be overwhelming. By choosing plants that have contrasting textures, you can create striking effects. Like color, texture helps set a mood. For example, an emphasis on bold, coarse-textured plants creates drama. Using fine-textured plants as the dominant partner in the mix creates a more restful landscape.

Leaf shape and size are an important part of texture. The typically small, narrow leaves of a fern, for example, have a fine texture. The wide, sometimes pleated leaves of a hosta have a coarse texture. Marrying the two in a shady border makes an eye-pleasing combination. You could also create a stunning scene simply by combining hostas of different shapes and sizes, from those with large, spoonlike leaves to others with narrow, dagger-shaped foliage.

The way the leaf feels to the touch is another important part of texture. A perennial such as bergenia has slick leaves, while the foliage of lamb's ears is soft and fuzzy. Foliage may also be crinkled, cushiony, spiny, fleshy, or hairlike. Consider the texture that flowers add to the garden, too. Dainty sprays of baby's breath or airy blooms of moor grass, for example, contrast nicely with the large, lush blossoms of roses or lilies.

The Function of Form

The shape, or form, of a plant plays an important part in garden design. When planning your landscape, consider each plant's characteristic growth habit—spiky, rounded, columnar, sprawling, fountainlike, or weeping. Use plants of contrasting shapes to balance and complement each other. By massing similar plants, you can accentuate their shape. Weeping specimens are best used as a focal point to call attention to their unusual form.

In addition to the overall shape of a plant, consider the shape of the flowers. Combine plants with contrasting flower form, whether spire, disk, globe, daisy, or plume, to add visual interest.

Size, a part of form, also deserves careful consideration. Otherwise, a plant may be out of proportion for the garden or require continual pruning to be pleasing to the eye. When planning a border, the time-honored rule of thumb dictates "tall in back, short in front." That's still good advice. But when you're creating a garden vignette, don't be afraid to break the rule. Small plants clustered around a taller, bulkier plant in the foreground, for example, could show off the contrast of forms and serve as an attractive accent.

ABOVE LEFT *Combining different plants of a single color can accentuate form. This silvery gray-green composition features cardoon (rear) and hummocks of lavender and lamb's ears.*

ABOVE RIGHT *Narrow spires of magenta liatris stand out among flat clusters of white yarrow, daisylike sunflowers, and purple coneflowers.*

BELOW *Slender columns of arborvitae create a harmonious backdrop for the broader-spreading cone shape of a dwarf Alberta spruce.*

FACING PAGE, INSET *In a simple contrast of textures, dense bloom clusters of Sedum 'Autumn Joy' are lightened by wispy plumes of feather reed grass (Calamagrostis × acutiflora).*

FACING PAGE, BOTTOM *Assemble a dramatic picture by making careful use of textural contrast: feathery celosia plumes, various wheel-like daisy blossoms, bold and broad canna foliage, and the narrow leaves of ornamental grass.*

Perennials

The word "perennial" means "returning again and again"—and that's just what perennial plants do. You plant them one year, and they persist in your garden to repeat their performance year after year. That's a major selling point for growing perennials. Unlike annuals, which must be planted each year, perennial plants can remain in place from several to many years.

Growth habits vary widely among plants in this group. Some remain totally evergreen, others decrease to small foliage mounds during the cold time of year, and still others disappear completely in winter but emerge anew the following spring. Among perennials, those with showy flowers are widely grown, but some choice perennials (hosta, for example) are cherished mainly for the beauty of their foliage.

Growing perennials does come with a few caveats. Some kinds are dependably perennial in favored climates but behave as annuals in others—so you'll need to know how a particular perennial will perform in your climate zone. When planting perennials, allow enough space for them to develop, and remember that some need several years to reach mature dimensions. Their flowering periods may be brief or fairly extended, but only a very few continue to bloom throughout spring and summer. If you want season-long color in a flower border, it's a good idea to mix generous amounts of annuals into the planting. And, of course, perennials do demand upkeep. All need yearly cleanup or cutting back for tidiness and some require periodic digging and dividing in order to remain vigorous.

LEFT *Purple coneflowers* (Echinacea purpurea), *black-eyed Susan* (Rudbeckia hirta), *wand loosestrife* (Lythrum virgatum), *and mealycup sage* (Salvia farinacea) *freely assort in this lavish Texas border.*

ABOVE LEFT *In late spring, Siberian irises display masses of flowers floating above clumps of grassy foliage. Leaves remain green throughout summer, then turn tawny russet in fall.*

ABOVE CENTER *Indestructible favorites, four o'clocks* (Mirabilis jalapa) *come in many colors; they open in late afternoon, perfuming the evening air.*

ABOVE RIGHT *Peonies have been garden favorites for well over a century. Their voluptuous, fragrant blooms appear in late spring on long-lived, shrubby plants.*

FOR HANDSOME FOLIAGE

All of these perennials have showy foliage throughout the growing season. Some also bear pretty flowers.

Autumn fern *Dryopteris erythrosora*
Cast-iron plant *Aspidistra elatior*
Christmas fern *Polystichum acrostichoides*
Evergreen candytuft *Iberis sempervirens*
Holly fern *Cyrtomium falcatum*
Hosta
Iris
Lamb's ears *Stachys byzantina*
Lenten rose *Helleborus orientalis*
Lily of China *Rohdea japonica*
Lily-of-the-Nile *Agapanthus*
Pink *Dianthus*
Thrift *Phlox subulata*
Wallflower *Erysimum* 'Bowles Mauve'
Yucca

FOR EXTENDED BLOOM

You can count on these perennials for showy flowers over a prolonged period.

Balloon flower *Platycodon grandiflorus*
Canna
Coreopsis
Firecracker plant *Russelia equisetiformis*
Four o'clock *Mirabilis jalapa*
French hollyhock *Malva sylvestris*
Gaura *Gaura lindheimeri*
Indian blanket *Gaillardia pulchella*
Mealycup sage *Salvia farinacea*
Mexican heather *Cuphea hyssopifolia*
Mexican petunia *Ruellia brittoniana*
ORNAMENTAL GRASSES
Pentas *Pentas lanceolata*
Perennial phlox *Phlox paniculata*
Purple coneflower *Echinacea purpurea*
Society garlic *Tulbaghia violacea*

Nature's Way

The Colonial South has its tradition of formal gardens, where clipped hedges corset orderly plantings of varied flowers. But away from the Colonial centers, another landscape style holds sway: the Southern cottage garden. These gardens are the antithesis of orderliness: colors and plant combinations freely mingle to form scenes of barely organized chaos.

Southern cottage gardens take their cue from classic English cottage gardens and from Southern rural custom: lawn is considered a waste of good soil, so every available square foot is devoted to flowers. Native perennials and biennials such as bee balm, gaura, and Queen Anne's lace are common components, often passed along from one gardener and family to another. Plants inclined to self-sow are allowed to pop up wherever they choose, even between stepping-stones. Though the initial planting may have had some sense of organization or adherence to a formula (such as "tall in back, short in front"), nature soon becomes the true designer.

To give it form, a cottage garden benefits from some sort of framework like an informal hedge, rustic fence, or wall. Some of these gardens may include an artistic focal point such as a fountain, sundial, or gazing globe—but the objective is to keep it simple. Sometimes even a brightly painted chair can add just the right finishing touch.

TOP *Thrusting their tightly packed spires of bloom skyward, foxgloves are a favorite cottage garden component for vertical accent. Biennial types are classic, so you need to set out new plants each year.*

MIDDLE *Warm and cool colors freely romp in this tapestry of perennials and shrubs. Strategically placed stepping-stones give access through the planting.*

RIGHT *A delightful hodgepodge of plants envelops a true cottage. Variety is the key to the planting's vitality, with only one design rule applying: "If you like it, plant it."*

ABOVE *Lack of water won't discourage fernleaf yarrow (foreground) or red-and-yellow blanket flower (background), but too much water can be destructive to these plants.*

LEFT *Orange butterfly weed (Asclepias tuberosa) and purple coneflower (Echinacea purpurea) need moderate watering at best, and easily endure drought and periods of capricious moisture.*

BELOW *Dry, gritty soil suits many plants from the Mediterranean region. This unthirsty planting features silver-leafed butterfly bush, verdant rosemary, yellow lemon thyme, and pink verbena.*

The Water Wise

Though most of the South gets all the rainfall it needs, water can be a precious commodity in parts of Oklahoma and Texas. Even in regions where average rainfall is adequate, the rain doesn't necessarily come when it's most needed—soil may be parched for weeks at a time in the hottest days of summer, just when plants demand adequate moisture for bloom and growth. And extended droughts often force communities in many areas to restrict outdoor watering just when gardens need water most.

Fortunately, many plants thrive with little water, once their root systems are established. Star performers include native perennials, such as butterfly weed *(Asclepias tuberosa),* autumn sage *(Salvia greggii),* and blanket flower *(Gaillardia × grandiflora).* These plants actually prefer dry weather and quickly decline if the soil stays too wet.

Many dry-soil plants come from the Mediterranean region, Australia, southern Africa, and Mexico, where dry summers are the norm. Bearded iris, cape plumbago *(Plumbago auriculata),* rosemary, bougainvillea, juniper, oleander, bear grass *(Nolina erumpens),* and lily-of-the-Nile *(Agapanthus)* are all exotic, drought-tolerant plants.

When choosing plants for a dry garden, look for those with gray or silvery foliage. Tiny hairs on the leaves and stems responsible for the color reduce transpiration and the need for added water. Also consider succulent plants, such as yuccas, sedums, and agaves.

Heavy, wet soil will rot the roots of many drought-tolerant plants. To improve drainage, till the bed to a depth of at least 12 inches before planting and add plenty of builder's sand, sharp gravel, ground bark, and expanded shale. Grade the bed so that excess rainfall runs off.

Bog Dwellers

It's true that you can't get plants to grow without water. But it's also true that you can have too much of a good thing. If you have clay soil in your garden that seems to take forever to dry, or a perpetually soggy meadow or boglike pond margin, you've no doubt discovered that saturated soil is relegated to the list of "garden problems." Why? Because the majority of favorite garden plants prefer a well-drained soil—one that can maintain the right balance of moisture and air to promote healthy root growth. For those plants, too much water leads to certain death, essentially by drowning.

If you're determined to beat the soggy soil situation, you can construct raised beds and fill them with soil heavily amended with organic matter. But there's another, simpler solution provided by none other than Mother Nature: grow plants that naturally *prefer* boggy areas that never dry out. Many plants take to soggy soil like a duck to water, and even some favorite perennials and shrubs that need "regular water" in the garden will also thrive in wet soil.

Among these "wet-feet" plants are some that actually will grow in soil that is submerged in a few inches of water. These are perfect choices for planting alongside a pond where water level may fluctuate according to rainfall and season, or in a low-lying area of the yard that collects moisture.

ABOVE *A backyard stream is artfully planted with a variety of damp-soil lovers. Prominent are white and yellow water irises (foreground) and spike-flowered pink Japanese primrose.*

TOP RIGHT *Florida anise* (Illicium floridanum) *is a handsome flowering shrub for damp, lightly shaded areas.*

MIDDLE RIGHT *Elegant Japanese irises* (Iris ensata) *feature saucer-size blooms over grassy-leafed plants suited to damp soil or shallow water.*

BOTTOM RIGHT *Uncommonly stylish blossoms of common calla reach perfection on plants grown in damp to boggy ground.*

FACING PAGE, TOP *Texas star* (Hibiscus coccineus).

FACING PAGE, CLOCKWISE FROM BOTTOM FAR LEFT *Yellow flag* (Iris pseudacorus), *Cardinal flower* (Lobelia cardinalis), *golden ray* (Ligularia stenocephala 'The Rocket'), *pitcher plants* (Sarracenia), *and black elephant's ear* (Colocasia esculenta 'Illustris').

WATER LOVERS

Perennials

Bee balm *Monarda didyma*
Blue flag* *Iris versicolor*
Bottle gentian *Gentiana andrewsii*
Canna (some)*
Cardinal flower* *Lobelia cardinalis*
Cinnamon fern *Osmunda cinnamomea*
Common calla *Zantedeschia aethiopica*
Elephant's ear* *Colocasia esculenta*
Forget-me-not *Myosotis scorpioides*
Globeflower *Trollius*
Golden ray *Ligularia*
Iris, Japanese and Louisiana*
Japanese coltsfoot *Petasites japonicus*
Japanese primrose* *Primula japonica*
Joe-Pye weed *Eupatorium purpureum*
Lady fern *Athyrium felix-femina*
Meadow sweet *Filipendula ulmaria*
Moor grass *Molinia caerulea*
New England aster *Aster novae-angliae*
Pitcher plant *Sarracenia*
Queen of the prairie *Filipendula rubra*
Rodgersia
Royal fern* *Osmunda regalis*
Southern blue flag* *Iris virginica*
Spiderwort *Tradescantia virginiana*
Sweet flag* *Acorus gramineus*
Texas star *Hibiscus coccineus*
Turtlehead *Chelone*
Yellow flag* *Iris pseudacorus*

Shrubs

Bog rosemary *Andromeda polifolia*
Buttonbush *Cephalanthus occidentalis*
Dwarf palmetto *Sabal minor*
Florida anise *Illicium floridanum*
Florida leucothoe *Agarista populifolia*
Inkberry *Ilex glabra*
Red chokeberry *Aronia arbutifolia*
Redtwig dogwood *Cornus sericea*
Summersweet *Clethra alnifolia*
Winterberry* *Ilex verticillata*

Trees

Black gum *Nyssa sylvatica*
River birch *Betula nigra*
Sweet bay *Magnolia virginiana*
Water oak *Quercus nigra*
Willow *Salix*

* Tolerate standing water

Annuals

Because annuals must be planted each year, gardeners may initially think they're too much trouble. But yearly planting is a small price to pay for the distinct advantages annuals possess. They provide instant color and, in many cases, bloom for months. They come in a near-endless array of forms and textures and in the full color spectrum. And if you don't like the choices one year, you can try new ones next year.

Depending on the type of weather they need in order to mature and bloom, annuals are separated into *cool-season* and *warm-season* categories. Cool-season annuals are planted in fall for bloom that may begin as early as late winter and extend into spring, until weather becomes too hot. Among these are larkspur, pansies and violas, pot marigold, Shirley poppy, sweet William, and decorative vegetables such as flowering cabbage and kale. Warm-season annuals are planted in spring for bloom from late spring until frost. Ageratum, impatiens, marigolds, and zinnias are familiar examples. Warm-season petunias are grown for summer bloom in most parts of the South, but in Florida they're planted in fall for flowers in winter.

In particular climates, some plants treated as annuals actually are perennials. Delphiniums, lupines, and snapdragons, for example, are perennials where summers are cool, but act as cool-season annuals in the South. Tropical perennials—such as coleus, Mexican heather, and pentas—are grown as perennials in frost-free regions but as annuals elsewhere.

In a word, annuals are *versatile.* You can use them for mass effect—in large groups or in broad swaths—or spot them in pots, hanging baskets, or window boxes. They're superb for filling the gaps in mixed borders and for providing seasonal color in perennial beds and rose gardens. For maximum impact, plant annuals in sizable groups (most are sold in cell-packs, making mass planting easy). Single-color blocks pack the most punch, but some annuals (such as bachelor's buttons, cosmos, Shirley poppies, and zinnias) are truly lovely in mixed colors. For more information on color combinations, see pages 158–159.

LEFT *Awash in color, this comfortable garden retreat is planted entirely with annuals—nature's premier plants for immediate results.*

FACING PAGE, TOP *Zinnias are summer standbys, with neon hues suggesting their south-of-the-border origin.*

FACING PAGE, MIDDLE *Easy-growing cosmos comes in pink, red, violet, lavender and white—simple daisy flowers backed by feathery foliage.*

FACING PAGE, BOTTOM *Early in the year, while temperatures are cool, larkspur delivers its trademark bloom spires in blue shades plus white and pink.*

FOR CUT FLOWERS

Calliopsis *Coreopsis tinctoria*
Celosia
Common cosmos
Larkspur *Consolida ajacis*
Pincushion flower *Scabiosa atropurpurea*
Pot marigold *Calendula officinalis*
Snapdragon *Antirrhinum majus*
Stock *Matthiola incana*
Sunflower *Helianthus annuus*
Sweet pea *Lathyrus odoratus*
Zinnia

FOR FRAGRANCE

English wallflower *Erysimum cheiri*
Flowering tobacco *Nicotiana*
Nasturtium *Tropaeolum majus*
Petunia
Stock *Matthiola incana*
Sweet alyssum *Lobularia maritima*
Sweet pea *Lathyrus odoratus*

FOR COLORED FOLIAGE

Castor bean *Ricinus communis* (some)
Coleus
Impatiens *Impatiens* New Guinea hybrids (some)
Perilla (some)
Snow-on-the-mountain *Euphorbia marginata*
Sweet basil *Ocimum basilicum* (some)
Wax begonia *Begonia* (semperflorens type)

Bulbs

Some of the South's best-loved garden flowers arise from bulbs—or from bulblike corms, tubers, rhizomes, or tuberous roots. Think of daffodils and tulips, irises and crinums. Bulbs are most commonly associated with eye-catching spring floral displays, but you also can find a number of bulbs that flower in summer, fall, or late winter.

Bulbs lend themselves to both formal and informal garden designs. Those that produce large blossoms atop long, sturdy stems—tulips and lilies, for example—tend to look better in orderly settings like mixed borders, mass plantings, or parterres. In contrast, those bulbs that increase freely, such as grape hyacinths, jonquils, Spanish bluebells, and spider lilies, can be naturalized in lawns, grassy meadows, and woodland gardens, where they'll gradually form loose drifts. Many of the spring-flowering bulbs are splendid container subjects for bursts of color on the terrace or patio.

While bulb blossoms are certainly showy, their display is somewhat fleeting; some flower for only about one week each year. There are, however, a few tricks you can use to extend the flowering period. With some bulbs (daffodils and tulips, in particular), you can mix early-, midseason-, and late-flowering varieties to extend the flowering period. And with some summer-blooming bulbs (such as gladiolus and calla), you can plant bulbs at two-week intervals in spring to get a succession of bloom in summertime. In a mixed border, you have the opportunity to include bulbs that bloom in each season.

To get the most visual punch from bulbs, plant them in masses. Groups of a single color have greatest impact, but combinations of related colors such as cream, yellow, orange, and red also are effective. In general, avoid the jumble of mixed-color plantings—the result usually is just floral confetti.

FACING PAGE *True to their name, magic lilies* (Lycoris squamigera) *suddenly appear in late summer, holding pink trumpets atop leafless stems.*

RIGHT *Dramatic cannas combine flamboyant flowers with bold foliage that may be green, variegated, or bronze.*

FAR RIGHT *Showy Louisiana irises come in a rainbow of colors and color combinations. Native to Southern swamplands, they also succeed in ordinary garden beds.*

BELOW *Fragrant paperwhite narcissus are cold hardy yet need no winter chill. Flowers come during winter in the South's milder regions.*

BELOW RIGHT *Tiger lilies are well-adapted to Southern climates; orange is the typical color, but newer kinds come in white, cream, pink, and red.*

Except for tulips, which are treated as annuals and discarded after flowering, spring-flowering bulbs need to remain in the ground after bloom until their foliage yellows and dies. If the bulbs are growing in a prominent spot, this calls for some measure of disguise. The simplest solution is to plant cool-weather annuals in fall in the space where bulbs lurk underground. In spring, the blooming annuals will conceal the yellowing bulb leaves. Low-growing evergreen ground covers such as common periwinkle can serve the same screening purpose.

OLD FAITHFULS

Some bulbs decline and fade away after a few years, but these Southern favorites will come back faithfully to bloom year after year.

Canna *
Common calla *Zantedeschia aethiopica*
Crinum *
Crocus
Daffodil *Narcissus*
Grape hyacinth *Muscari*
Iris (Louisiana and Siberian)

Lily-of-the-valley *Convallaria majalis*
Magic lily, spider lily *Lycoris*
Montbretia *Crocosmia crocosmiiflora*
Snowflake *Leucojum*
Spanish bluebell *Hyacinthoides hispanica*
Tiger lily *Lilium lancifolium*
Yellow flag *Iris pseudacorus*

* Not winter-hardy in all parts of the South

171

Edibles in the Landscape

Once upon a time, plants that were grown for their produce were relegated to the vegetable patch out back, leaving *the garden* for flowers and other ornamentals. While this separation was an efficient arrangement—especially when large quantities of edibles were being grown—it also managed to imply that edibles were not attractive enough to mingle with mainstream garden beauties. But today's gardeners know better. As contemporary garden areas have shrunk (making a dedicated vegetable garden something of a luxury) and adventurous gardeners have experimented with avant-garde plant combinations, edibles have taken root in the general landscape.

Combining edible and ornamental plants in the garden simply makes good sense. Why relegate Swiss chard or rhubarb, for example, to the garden's outer limits, when their foliage is just as handsome as that of many ornamental plants? Woven into the general landscape, they—and a host of other vegetables, fruits, and herbs—can hold their own as pretty faces while still working hard to manufacture food. And if you have a small yard, interplanting edibles and ornamentals means that you don't have to choose between these two worlds. You can have a landscaped garden and produce, too.

Whether you create a flower garden with edibles or a vegetable garden with flowers depends entirely on the requirements you have and the emphasis you want. The photographs on these pages prove that either approach can lead to a garden that is both beautiful and productive.

TOP *Rosettes of cabbage and frilly heads of lettuce mix with spring daffodils.*

RIGHT *Edible and ornamental plants are thoroughly integrated in this well-crafted mixed border.*

LEFT *Edibles hug the left side of a path, while annuals and perennials decorate the right.*

BELOW *A scarecrow couple hovers over a huge pumpkin as if to say, "We grew it ourselves!"*

BOTTOM RIGHT *Tulips and pot marigolds* (Calendula) *add early-spring panache to cool-season edibles.*

Herb Potpourri

Herbs are indispensable to cooks and to their culinary efforts. But herb plants with their varied textures, hues, and scents, also can add considerable spice to gardens. In this Homewood, Alabama, garden, herbs consort with lettuce and a potpourri of flowers to create a patchwork planting as pleasing to the eye as to the palate.

The first step in making this garden was finding the right location—one with well-drained soil and at least four hours of sunlight each day. Meeting the sunlight requirement was a simple matter. But with less-than-perfect soil, good drainage could only be achieved by amending the soil with organic matter.

With the soil suitably prepared, it was time to choose the plants—and not just ordinary, store-available fare but unusual kinds of herbs and vegetables from specialty-seed houses. As a result, the garden brims over with several fancy varieties of basil and leaf lettuce. Pots provide for the drier soil preferred by some herbs such as silver thyme and golden oregano. Containers also elevate and display to advantage low-growing herbs among their taller, more rambunctious neighbors.

Cape plumbago, Madagascar periwinkle, and narrow-leaf zinnia contribute bouquets of bright color to this handsome arrangement of vegetable and herb foliage. Stonework edgings keep beds in place and repeat the stone borders used in other parts of the garden.

ABOVE *Growing some herbs in pots lets you highlight those plants while adding a bit of visual interest to the planting.*

LEFT *An edging of native stone defines the beds, yet still allows plants to attractively spill out onto the path.*

FACING PAGE *Dense planting allows you to grow many different herbs in a relatively small space. A pathway cuts through and around, making harvesting easy.*

Ornamental Grasses

In the South, where manicured lawns are a way of life, ornamental grasses represent a less familiar concept: grasses you don't mow! But there's no denying the beauty these carefree kin to lawn grasses add to the landscape. Most form fountainlike clumps—some more upright (like shaving brushes), others more relaxed (like haystacks). From these clumps rise stems bearing showy plumes of tiny flowers that mature to decorative seed heads. Green is the standard leaf color, but some kinds have distinctly bluish foliage or leaves striped in yellow, cream, or white. Many ornamental grasses develop outstanding fall color that can last through winter, providing the plants aren't battered by storms.

The soft, billowy style of ornamental grasses makes them natural choices for informal plantings and naturalized areas. Many also are perfect for the beach or water's edge. In small gardens, choose size carefully and use these showy grasses as accent specimens. Where more space is available, you can use them freely in mixed borders—even to the extent of making entire planting beds of grass. The taller kinds (such as maiden, pampas, and ravenna grasses) can be planted as informal screens. One annual cleanup takes care of maintenance: rake away dead leaves and flower stems of deciduous kinds and cut back clumps of evergreen types.

Ornamental grasses include a few attractive kinds that unfortunately are prone to bad behavior in the garden. Maiden grass and river oats, for instance, can self-sow to the point of becoming a nuisance. And those that spread by underground runners—giant reed grass, ribbon grass, and running (as opposed to clumping) bamboos—should be avoided entirely.

LEFT *Ornamental grasses contribute their own unique autumnal hues to a warm tapestry of fall colors. Chinese pennisetum provides a border of contrasting straw color along the green lawn. Rusty-red plumes of maiden grass rise behind the border.*

AN ORNAMENTAL GRASS SAMPLER

NAME	LIGHT	HEIGHT	DESCRIPTION/COMMENTS/ZONES*
Blue fescue *Festuca glauca*	Sun/part shade	4–11 in.	Forms blue-gray tufts. Useful for edging, massing, accents. Best in zones US and MS.
Blue oat grass *Helictotrichon sempervirens*	Sun	2–3 ft.	Clumping grass looks like a much-enlarged blue fescue, with bright blue-gray leaves in fountainlike clumps. Straw-colored flower plumes in spring rise above foliage mass. Evergreen to semievergreen. US, MS, LS, and CS.
Chinese pennisetum *Pennisetum alopecuroides*	Sun/part shade	2–4 ft.	Plumes can be tan, white, or dark purple, depending on selection; yellow or orange fall foliage. Use with perennials or in solid borders. Very dependable in US, MS, LS, and CS.
Feather reed grass *Calamagrostis × acutiflora*	Sun	3–4 ft.	Bright green foliage. Tall, erect flower spikes quite showy. Makes splendid vertical accent; effective in masses. 'Karl Foerster' is the selection usually sold. Grows in LS, CS; blooms best in US and MS.
Fountain grass *Pennisetum* 'Burgundy Giant'	Sun	4–5 ft.	Handsome burgundy foliage with showy red-purple plumes. Makes striking color accent. Annual in US, MS, and LS; perennial in CS and TS.
Gulf muhly *Muhlenbergia filipes*	Sun/part shade	4–5 ft.	Clumping native grass, spectacular in fall as wispy plumes held above foliage turn reddish pink. Tolerates poor, dry soil. MS, LS, CS, and TS.
Japanese sedge *Carex morrowii*	Shade/part shade	1 ft.	Small, mounding plant good for edging, rock gardens, mixed borders, containers. Likes moist soil; effective near water. Variegated forms have gold- or white-striped leaves. US, MS, LS, and CS.
Lindheimer's muhly *Muhlenbergia lindheimeri*	Sun/part shade	3–5 ft.	Showy, silvery gray plumes stand atop narrow, blue-green leaves in fall. Nice textural accent; good for naturalized areas; tolerates wet or dry soil. MS, LS, CS, and TS.
Little bluestem *Schizachyrium scoparium*	Sun/part shade	2–3 ft.	Clumping grass with blue-green leaves that turn coppery red in fall. Good for naturalizing, but will self-sow. Tolerates wet or dry soil. US, MS, LS, and CS.
Maiden grass *Miscanthus sinensis* 'Gracillimus'	Sun/part shade	5–6 ft.	Slender weeping foliage with narrow, white midrib; reddish plumes; leaves orange in fall. Forms large clump. Use in mixed borders, near water, or as informal screen. Dependable in US, MS, LS, and CS.
Oriental fountain grass *Pennisetum orientale*	Sun/part shade	1–1½ ft.	Clumping grass topped with pinkish plumes. Front of the border plant; good choice for massing or mixing with perennials in US, MS, LS, and CS.
Pampas grass *Cortaderia selloana*	Sun	8–12 ft.	Clumping grass with showy, large white plumes in summer. Use as accent or informal screen. Withstands salt and wind. Best in MS, LS, CS, TS.
Ravenna grass *Saccharum ravennae*	Sun	10–15 ft.	Large clump of gray-green leaves topped by silvery plumes in late summer. Not as showy as pampas grass, but hardier to cold. Use as large accent or informal screen. All zones.
River oats *Chasmanthium latifolium*	Sun/part shade	2–4 ft.	Clumping grass crowned by seed heads that resemble flattened clusters of oats; good textural accent. Grows in almost any situation; self-sows rampantly. US, MS, LS, and CS.
Switch grass *Panicum virgatum*	Sun/part shade	4–5 ft.	Clumping native grass with blue-green leaves that turn red or yellow in fall; airy clouds of pinkish blooms in summer. Takes wet or dry soil. Use as accent or in masses in US, MS, and LS.

Upper South (US), Middle South (MS), Lower South (LS), Coastal South (CS), Tropical South (TS)

Maiden grass

Gulf muhly

Blue fescue

Pampas grass

Nectar Sweet

Can a garden have too much color? Butterflies and hummingbirds would seem to say "No," as they flit about, embellishing your planned color display with serendipitous hues. Think of a ruby-throated hummingbird probing a ruby red penstemon or a tiger swallowtail butterfly sunning itself on a head of yarrow blossoms. What else could offer such garden adornment and entertainment?

Hosting butterfly and hummingbird visitors involves a certain amount of luck, but you can improve your odds if you include some of their favorite plants in your garden. The secret to luring these creatures is twofold: color and nectar. Hummingbirds zero in on red, orange, pink, and blue, favoring plants in those colors that *also* feature tubular flowers into which they can plunge their needlelike beaks. Butterflies have a more cosmopolitan color taste, but initially may be drawn by brightness—and, once attracted, will shop around for nectar.

In the South, there's no shortage of nectar-rich shrubs, perennials, and annuals to entice hummingbirds and butterflies. From the lists on the facing page you'll find plants that flower in spring, summer, and autumn; include some for each season to ensure the longest possible parade of these winged visitors.

ABOVE LEFT, INSET *A monarch butterfly uses a flat-topped cluster of yarrow flowers as a landing pad.*

TOP *Hummingbirds can't resist the tube-shaped blossoms of* Agastache *'Desert Sunrise'.*

ABOVE *A tiger swallowtail butterfly extracts nourishing nectar from a purple coneflower.*

ABOVE RIGHT *Butterfly weed lives up to its name, luring a great spangled fritillary.*

FACING PAGE, TOP *Blue flowers—especially those with tubular throats—are practically guaranteed to attract hummingbirds.*

FACING PAGE, BOTTOM *A Gulf fritillary makes a "fueling" pit-stop on a cluster of lantana blossoms before takeoff.*

BUTTERFLY LURES

Shrubs

Butterfly bush *Buddleia*
Buttonbush *Cephalanthus occidentalis*
Chaste tree *Vitex*
Glossy abelia *Abelia × grandiflora*
Honeysuckle *Lonicera*
Lantana
Spirea *Spiraea*
Summersweet *Clethra alnifolia*

Perennials

Aster
Beard tongue *Penstemon*
Black-eyed Susan *Rudbeckia hirta*
Blanket flower *Gaillardia*
Blazing star *Liatris*
Butterfly weed *Asclepias tuberosa*
Columbine *Aquilegia*
Common ginger lily
   Hedychium coronarium
Coreopsis
Goldenrod *Solidago*
Joe-Pye weed *Eupatorium purpureum*
Phlox
Purple coneflower *Echinacea purpurea*
Sage *Salvia*
Shasta daisy
   Chrysanthemum maximum
Stonecrop *Sedum* (tall kinds)
Valerian *Centranthus ruber*
Yarrow *Achillea*

Annuals

Calliopsis *Coreopsis tinctoria*
Common cosmos *Cosmos bipinnatus*
Cupid's dart *Catananche caerulea*
Dame's rocket *Hesperis matronalis*
Globe amaranth *Gomphrena globosa*
Impatiens
Marigold *Tagetes*
Mexican sunflower *Tithonia*
   rotundifolia
Pentas *Pentas lanceolata*
Pincushion flower
   Scabiosa atropurpurea
Queen Anne's lace
   Daucus carota carota
Snapdragon *Antirrhinum majus*
Spider flower *Cleome hasslerana*
Sweet alyssum *Lobularia maritima*

HUMMINGBIRD MAGNETS

Shrubs, Vines

Beauty bush *Kolkwitzia amabilis*
Butterfly bush *Buddleia*
Cape honeysuckle *Tecoma capensis*
Glossy abelia *Abelia × grandiflora*
Honeysuckle *Lonicera*
Lantana
Texas ranger *Leucophyllum frutescens*
Weigela *Weigela floribunda*

Perennials

Agastache
Beard tongue *Penstemon*
Bee balm *Monarda didyma*
Butterfly weed *Asclepias tuberosa*
Canna
Cape fuchsia *Phygelius*
Cardinal flower *Lobelia cardinalis*
Columbine *Aquilegia*
Coral bells *Heuchera*
Delphinium
Four o'clock *Mirabilis jalapa*
Foxglove *Digitalis*
Hollyhock *Alcea rosea*
Red-hot poker *Kniphofia*
Sage *Salvia*
Tiger lily *Lilium lancifolium*

Annuals

Annual phlox *Phlox drummondii*
Flowering tobacco *Nicotiana*
Impatiens
Nasturtium *Tropaeolum majus*
Petunia
Scarlet sage *Salvia splendens*
Snapdragon *Antirrhinum majus*
Zinnia

Wildflowers

Gardens of Southern wildflowers celebrate the diversity of our region's native plants. From the wide range of choices, you can invite a few select wildflowers into a garden of established non-native (exotic) flora or express purely regional pride in a naturalistic garden composed entirely of Southern wildflowers.

Many native annuals reseed prolifically, making them ideal for naturalizing at garden fringes, on hillsides, and along roadsides. Bluebonnet, calliopsis, annual phlox, Indian paintbrush, and Indian blanket are prime examples. Showy perennials like goldenrod, gaura, and orange coneflower are tough, dependable performers well suited for use in mixed and perennial borders. Quite a few Southern wildflowers prefer the moist, rich soil and dappled shade of a woodland garden, showing off well beneath limbed-up trees or at

the edge of a forest's tree canopy. Favorites among these include blue phlox, Virginia bluebells, and wild columbine.

The concept of a wildflower meadow is alluring, but in the South it seldom is a self-sustaining proposition. The first year from seeding may generate a floral display, but our ample rainfall and long growing season encourage grasses and other weeds that will smother most wildflower meadows in short order. If you want to have a flowering meadow, be prepared to till the soil and scatter fresh seed every year.

ABOVE *Columbines* (Aquilegia) *are champion reseeders, popping up randomly year after year. Here, their lavish spring blooms swarm around a wellhead.*

A WILDFLOWER SAMPLER

NAME	LIGHT	BLOOM	DESCRIPTION/ZONES*
Annual phlox *Phlox drummondii*	Sun	Summer and fall	Showy clusters of pink, white, rose, salmon, or red flowers; grows 6–18 in. tall; reseeding annual. All zones.
Bachelor's button *Centaurea cyanus*	Sun	Summer	Annual grown mainly for cut flowers in blue, pink, rose, wine red, or white; also called "cornflower." Easy to grow; reaches 2½ ft. tall. All zones.
Blue phlox *Phlox divaricata*	Sun/light shade	Spring	Blue to purple flowers; spreads by seed; grows 6–12 in. tall; perennial. US, MS, LS, CS.
Calliopsis *Coreopsis tinctoria*	Sun	Spring	Yellow, orange, maroon, bronze, or burgundy flowers atop wiry stems; grows 1½–3 ft. tall; reseeding annual. All zones.
Cardinal flower *Lobelia cardinalis*	Sun/part shade	Summer	Spikes of bright red flowers; attracts hummingbirds; needs moist or wet soil; grows 2–4 ft. high; perennial. US, MS, LS, CS.
Gaura *Gaura lindheimeri*	Sun	Spring to fall	White or pink flowers borne on long, thin stems; self-sows; tolerates drought; grows 2–4 ft. high; perennial. US, MS, LS, CS.
Goldenrod *Solidago*	Sun	Late summer through fall	Showy yellow flowers; many species; doesn't cause hayfever; grows 2–7 ft.; perennial. US, MS, LS, CS.
Indian blanket *Gaillardia pulchella*	Sun	Spring to fall	Red, yellow, and maroon daisylike flowers; tolerates poor soil, drought; grows 1½–2 ft. high; reseeding annual. All zones.
Indian paintbrush *Castilleja indivisa*	Sun	Spring	Showy orange and red flower spikes; thrives in poor, dry soil; grows 6–16 in. tall; reseeding annual. All zones.
Joe-Pye weed *Eupatorium purpureum*	Sun/light shade	Late summer and fall	Large clusters of dusty rose flowers; attracts butterflies; grows 3–9 ft. tall; perennial. US, MS, LS, CS.
Orange coneflower *Rudbeckia fulgida*	Sun/light shade	Summer	Orange-yellow, daisylike blooms; often called black-eyed Susan; grows 3–4 ft. tall; perennial. US, MS, LS, CS.
Swamp sunflower *Helianthus angustifolius*	Sun	Late summer and fall	Showy, bright yellow, daisylike blooms; tolerates wet or well-drained soil; may be invasive; 5–10 ft. tall; perennial. US, MS, LS, CS.
Texas bluebonnet *Lupinus texensis*	Sun	Spring	Spikes of blue flowers with white centers that turn red; prefers dry, poor, rocky soil; grows 1 ft. tall; reseeding annual. MS, LS, CS.
Virginia bluebells *Mertensia virginica*	Part shade/shade	Spring	Pink flower buds open to bright blue flowers; needs moist, fertile soil; grows 1–2 ft. tall; perennial. US, MS, LS.
Wild columbine *Aquilegia canadensis*	Sun/light shade	Spring	Nodding flowers in orange-red and yellow; reseeds; needs moist, fertile soil; grows 1–2 ft. tall; short-lived perennial. US, MS, LS.
Wild foxglove *Penstemon cobaea*	Part shade	Mid- to late spring	Perennial; showy clusters of tubular flowers in white or lavender with deeper colored throats. Takes regular to little water; grows to 2½ ft. tall. US, MS, LS, CS.

Upper South (US), Middle South (MS), Lower South (LS), Coastal South (CS), Tropical South (TS)

Blue phlox

Wild columbine

Gaura

Wild foxglove

A Taste of the Tropics

Tropical and subtropical plants are no strangers to gardens in the Coastal and Tropical South, and they're gaining popularity in the more northerly reaches of the South as well. This comes as no surprise. Once seen, these plants simply sell themselves. Who wouldn't be attracted to spectacular blooms and lush, bold foliage? Best of all, these plants thrive in the warm, humid climate common to so much of the South. Freezing temperatures are their nemesis, but a surprising number will tolerate a drop in temperature below 32°F.

These denizens of the tropics are guaranteed successes as accent specimens—and when combined with more traditional "northerly" plants, they'll give any garden an exotic look. In fact, a combination of plants with different shapes and sizes of leaves can be just as dramatic and attractive as a mixture of different kinds of flowers. For greatest impact, go for contrast. You can juxtapose large, coarse leaves with small, delicate foliage. Or you might try contrasting plants with dark or bronzy leaves to those with foliage that is light green or variegated.

Even cold winters need not dampen your enthusiasm for growing tropical plants. In the Lower South, a heavy mulch applied in fall can be enough to guarantee winter survival for many of these plants. And where that won't suffice, you can grow them in containers that you take indoors for shelter over winter. Even something as large as a banana tree can be preserved indoors. Just dig up the plant in fall, cut off its leaves and much of the trunk, then store it in a cool, dark, non-freezing spot until temperatures are consistently warm enough for replanting outdoors.

FACING PAGE, TOP LEFT *Passion flowers embody the essence of tropical flora.*

ABOVE LEFT *Giant alocasia (Alocasia macrorrhiza) sets an indisputably tropical tone in this lavish porchside border.*

FACING PAGE, BOTTOM *The intense colors of a variegated canna, huge leaves of castor bean (Ricinus communis), and brilliant orange of Mexican sunflower (Tithonia rotundifolia) combine to represent "tropical" at its most exuberant.*

TOP RIGHT *Caladiums display vibrant colors and dramatic leaf shape—two quintessential tropical attributes.*

ABOVE *Neon-bright bougainvillea comes in all classic tropical colors.*

LEFT *Foliage carries the tropical motif here, with a stand of bananas, massed caladiums, and potted cycads.*

Fall Display

Autumn may well be the South's most pleasant season, and it's certainly one of the most colorful. But with the exception of beautyberry *(Callicarpa),* chrysanthemums, firethorn *(Pyracantha),* winged euonymus, and sasanqua camellias, few plants are grown for their autumn display alone. Most are prized mainly for their spring or summer bloom, with late-season color coming as an added bonus. Among these "fall-dividend" plants are many Southern favorite trees and shrubs, including bottlebrush buckeye *(Aesculus parviflora),* flowering crabapple *(Malus),* crepe myrtle *(Lagerstroemia indica),* flowering dogwood *(Cornus florida),* oakleaf hydrangea *(Hydrangea quercifolia),* pomegranate, sourwood *(Oxydendrum arboreum),* and several viburnums. Among perennials, numerous ornamental grasses stand out for their showy summer blooms that fade to buff in fall or for their tawny or reddish autumn leaves.

Should you set out to plant a garden for fall color, consider these few guidelines. Pay attention to leaf color: avoid placing plants with pinkish red foliage next to those with orange-red leaves—the colors just don't get along. And try to use the green of lawns, ground covers, and evergreen shrubs to showcase the autumn colors; with green for contrast, the bright, warm shades appear especially vibrant. Finally, remember that brilliant fall foliage isn't a yearly guarantee in the South. In addition to the multi-season beauties mentioned above, the most dependable and consistent autumn hues among trees without showy flowers come from American beech *(Fagus grandifolia),* Chinese pistache *(Pistacia chinensis),* hickory *(Carya),* Japanese maple *(Acer palmatum),* red maple *(Acer rubrum* 'October Glory'), sassafras *(Sassafras albidum),* and sugar maple *(Acer saccharum).*

If you live in the Coastal or Tropical South (where autumn foliage is mainly green), use flowers for fall color. Pansies and violas, petunias, pot marigold, and sweet alyssum are sure bets.

FACING PAGE *Chinese pistache* (Pistacia chinensis) *is a valuable shade tree that sets the autumn landscape ablaze with yellow, orange, red, or maroon—even in mild-winter regions.*

TOP *Fall-blooming perennial asters reliably deliver masses of bloom in the blue and purple tones so rare at the close of the year.*

ABOVE LEFT *Like a tower of molten gold, native shagbark hickory* (Carya ovata) *lights up the autumn scene.*

ABOVE RIGHT *Berry clusters of heavenly bamboo* (Nandina domestica) *turn red in time for fall display, then remain colorful right through winter.*

BELOW *Fairly glowing in the soft light of autumn, pineapple sage* (Salvia elegans) *makes a splash in fire-engine red.*

Winter Accents

In winter, the South becomes two garden worlds: the Tropical South, where green leaves and flowers abound, and everywhere else. It is for "everywhere else" that color and form are of paramount interest in the chilliest, darkest time of year.

Liberal plantings of evergreen trees and shrubs give Southern gardens considerable "life" during winter, alleviating any sense of bleakness. And with those evergreens to establish the garden's form and provide a backdrop, winter flowers, fruits, and bare limbs show off to great effect.

Berried plants give the longest-lasting winter color display. Classic Southern berry producers are hollies,

including evergreen kinds such as winterberry (*Ilex verticillata*) and deciduous types like possumhaw (*I. decidua*). Most are shrubby plants, but in time some become small trees. Other reliable berry producers are crabapple *(Malus)*, hawthorn *(Crataegus)*, heavenly bamboo *(Nandina domestica)*, and some viburnums.

A surprising number of shrubs and trees flower at some point during winter. Trees include Japanese flowering apricot *(Prunus mume),* 'Okame' flowering cherry *(Prunus* 'Okame'), purple orchid tree *(Bauhinia variegata),* star and saucer magnolias *(Magnolia stellata* and *M. × soulangeana),* and Taiwan flowering cherry

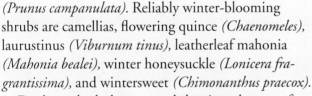

(Prunus campanulata). Reliably winter-blooming shrubs are camellias, flowering quince *(Chaenomeles)*, laurustinus *(Viburnum tinus)*, leatherleaf mahonia *(Mahonia bealei)*, winter honeysuckle *(Lonicera fragrantissima)*, and wintersweet *(Chimonanthus praecox)*.

Don't overlook the more subtle winter beauty of decorative bark, colored stems, and sculptural shapes of bare plants. Especially with good background evergreens for contrast, you can appreciate the patch-work bark of crepe myrtles, the showy twigs of several shrubby dogwoods, and the intricate, tiered limb structure of Japanese maples.

FACING PAGE *There's no shortage of bloom in this late-winter garden. Lenten rose* (Helleborus orientalis) *borders a path leading past a flowering quince* (Chaenomeles *hybrid*).

FACING PAGE, INSET *Catkins adorn the branches of Harry Lauder's walking stick* (Corylus avellana *'Contorta'*).

TOP LEFT *Crepe myrtle's decorative bark lends a subtle touch of color to the winter scene.*

CENTER LEFT *Bright stems of yellowtwig dogwood* (Cornus sericea *'Flaviramea'*) *show off after leaves drop in fall.*

LOWER LEFT *Elegant camellia blossoms can be counted on to brighten Southern gardens throughout winter.*

TOP RIGHT *Winter snow transforms a leafless flowering dogwood into a silvery ice sculpture.*

ABOVE RIGHT *Long-lasting fruits of flowering crabapple look like tiny holiday ornaments on the tree's bare branches.*

CHAPTER 5

Finishing Touches

Nothing is more completely the child of art than a garden.

—Sir Walter Scott

Containers

Whether it's a little box of herbs by the kitchen door, a pair of dramatic potted ferns on the front porch, or pots filled with seasonal blooms in the garden, the time-honored tradition of growing plants in containers lets you garden just about anywhere. Any container that holds soil can be home to plants, but holes for good drainage are a must (place a piece of screen or other tough, porous material over the drainage holes to keep soil in but let water out). Where winter freezes are common, don't plant in terra-cotta pots unless you plan on bringing them in

TOP RIGHT *A moss-lined basket overflowing with fragrant annuals makes a perfect outdoor centerpiece.*

RIGHT *This elegant footed bowl brims with delectable lemon-scented herbs.*

BELOW *To unify pots of different shapes, colors, and sizes, plant them with similar flowers—like these mums in shades of pink.*

BELOW RIGHT *For variations on a theme, choose classic urns fashioned from (left to right) rustic iron, terra-cotta, and concrete.*

for winter, as ice will crack them. Fragile containers, including those made of wood, will last a lot longer if they have some protection from the elements. If overall weight is an issue, such as on a deck or balcony, choose pots made of plastic or other lightweight synthetic material.

Be prepared to water some container plantings often, especially in hot, dry, or windy weather. Locate

pots near a water source, or install permanent drip lines to make this task as easy as possible.

When choosing a container, remember that the more ornate the pot, the simpler its contents should be. Or leave a stunning container empty and let it stand as a piece of garden art.

TOP *An old shoeshine box in soft green is an ideal display case for small containers of flowers and herbs.*

ABOVE *A chocolate-colored pot holds a confection of pink begonias, petunias, and geraniums, all topped by a frosting of white caladiums and variegated dracaena.*

TOP RIGHT *Blooming in a pebble-filled birdbath, these fragrant paperwhite narcissus are conveniently elevated to nose level.*

RIGHT *Turn an old chair into a whimsical garden in a few simple steps: replace the seat with chicken wire (secured by staples), line with sphagnum moss or cocoa fiber, and fill with potting soil and low-growing herbs.*

Finishing Touches

ABOVE *Holding their own against the vivid blue glaze of this container are gazanias, euryops, dahlias, lilies, and sunflowers in blazing hues.*

TOP RIGHT *A graceful terra-cotta pot holds a charming green-and-pink planting of soft maidenhair fern* (Adiantum) *and fluffy lace-cap hydrangeas.*

BOTTOM RIGHT *Why stop at ground level? Carry a floral theme (like these bright impatiens) right up a post, with the help of pots held securely in metal cages.*

BELOW *Two-level loveliness: training a yellow-flowered abutilon into a standard makes room for colorful crotons* (Codiaeum variegatum pictum) *and begonias beneath.*

LEFT *Stylish cousins of the plain clay pot, these containers flaunt basket weave and fancy floral designs.*

BELOW LEFT *To keep a strawberry pot well irrigated, cut a piece of PVC pipe almost to the pot's height, drill it all over with ⅛-inch holes, cap it at the bottom, and set it upright in the pot before planting. To add water and liquid fertilizer, just fill the pipe.*

BELOW *Pretty and practical, glazed Italian cachepots sparkle with color.*

BOTTOM *A double-decker planter is filled with flowering kale, pansies, and dusty miller for a colorful fall show.*

Window Gardens

You can bring your garden nearly indoors with a well-planted window box. And growing plants in a window box, sling, or rack is just as easy as gardening in any other type of container. While mass plantings of a single flower can look lovely beneath a window, mixed plantings are usually the showstoppers. Try combining a variety of upright, bushy, and trailing plants in a "windowscape." Make sure all the plants will thrive in the amount of light that the box receives throughout the day.

Window boxes may be wood, plastic, or metal. (A plastic or metal liner will protect a wooden box and make planting and care easier.) All should have openings for good drainage. Attach window boxes and other planters with heavy-duty hardware; if not properly supported, they could become a safety hazard.

TOP *A vine-draped basket displays blue and white cape plumbago, creeping Jenny (Lysimachia nummularia), artemisia, rex begonias, and variegated vinca.*

ABOVE *Old metal sap buckets painted and cleverly arranged contain petunias, basil, and deep purple 'Blackie' ornamental sweet potato.*

LEFT *Unpainted wooden boxes look charmingly rustic. Build them from rot-resistant wood, such as redwood, cedar, teak, or pressure-treated pine.*

ABOVE *Simply elegant in winter, this window box features annual ryegrass planted among loops of dried vines. In spring, the grass is replaced with blooming annuals.*

BELOW LEFT *Boxwoods shaped like holiday trees, pink impatiens, and an ivy swag create a formal yet festive composition.*

BELOW RIGHT *A metal hayrack holds a simple cocoa-fiber liner filled with pretty petunias and other colorful annuals.*

Birdhouses

Nothing says "friendly" like a birdhouse in the garden—especially if it's brightly colored, uniquely designed, or whimsical in style. But if you want to invite winged visitors to stay a spell, a birdhouse needs to be constructed as suitable lodging, too.

Before you go shopping or grab the toolbox, you need to decide what kind of birdhouse you want. Do you want the birdhouse to function primarily as a garden ornament? Or will it be a welcoming hostel for live-in guests?

Only birds that nest in tree hollows need houses. Small birds like chickadees and nuthatches prefer an entry hole that is $1\frac{1}{8}$ inches across. Medium-size birds like swallows need a nest box with a hole of $1\frac{1}{2}$ inches. White-breasted nuthatches need $1\frac{1}{4}$ inches. Larger birds such as flickers require $2\frac{1}{2}$-inch entry holes.

Bluebirds have strict building codes. Their houses must be 6 inches wide, 6 inches deep, 9 to 12 inches high, and about 4 feet off the ground with an entry hole $1\frac{1}{2}$ inches wide. The best color? Bright blue. Of course, a house with dimensions to suit a bluebird will likely attract other birds of similar size as well.

A. This campground of rustic cabins offers visitor lodging on a first-come, first-occupied basis. The tin roof of the unit in the foreground is a recycled license plate.

B. Apartments available! This plush complex offers all the conveniences of modern avian living.

C. The roof of this two-story house, made from a rusted sign, keeps living quarters and occupants dry.

D. What safer place to live than a cathedral? Though towering, it houses a cozy nest box inside its walls.

C   D

Basic Housekeeping

To thwart raccoons and cats, mount birdhouses atop metal poles or hang them from tree branches.

Place birdhouses away from bird feeders (feeding frenzies make nesting birds nervous).

Face the entry toward the south or east, but in any case away from prevailing winds and hot afternoon sun.

When setting a birdhouse on a metal pole, fit it with a metal squirrel baffle at least 16 inches wide to discourage squirrels and protect baby birds from black rat snakes.

Build with an insulating material such as 1-inch-thick wood. Thinner materials, such as plastic, ventilate poorly and can get too hot.

Nest boxes need to have a side or top that opens, so that the box can be cleaned. They also need drain holes in the bottom and ventilation holes high in the sides.

Birdbaths

Water is a real magnet for birds. Place a simple dish of clean water in your garden, and they won't be able to pass it by. Add a birdbath or two, especially one fitted with a bubbling fountain, and your garden will become a popular—and frequent— resort for feathered visitors of all kinds.

You can design and craft your own birdbath or purchase one from an array of styles available. Hanging types can be suspended from tree limbs, giving *you* a bird's-eye view of avian antics and *them* an elevated spa in which to play.

Location is key to protecting birds from raptors and feline hunters. A wet bird is less able to escape predators (see "Foil predators" on the facing page). Birds love shallow water, but remember that it heats quickly on hot days and in direct sun. Choose a spot shaded from midday and late afternoon sun.

Whatever type of birdbath you choose, keep it clean and filled. Even in winter, birds need water to wet their whistles—and for bathing too, so their feathers remain clean and fluffed for maximum warmth.

FACING PAGE, INSET *A simple sunflower, captured in metal, offers birds a chance to bathe in high style.*

FACING PAGE *An ornate column supports a shallow pool made from a ceramic urn saucer.*

NEAR RIGHT *In this minimalist-modern birdbath, recirculating water bubbles over a stylized stone in a celadon green "pool."*

WATER SPOTS

TOP LEFT *Cast concrete gives non-slip footing that's just to the birds' liking.*

TOP RIGHT *Assembled in an instant, this birdbath consists only of a glazed saucer atop a large terra-cotta pot.*

ABOVE LEFT *Animation, suspended: place a hanging birdbath where you can see birds' frolicking and preening.*

ABOVE RIGHT *A birdbath-size pond in the hollow of a boulder offers the ultimate in naturalism.*

LEFT *Birds likely enjoy splashing water in the faces of these sculpted peeping Toms.*

Birdbaths 101

Select the right type. Stone, concrete, and ceramic make fine birdbaths. If you opt for metal, make it stainless steel for rust resistance. And if you have heavy frost in your area, make sure the bath can handle the cold by adding a heating element to keep the water from freezing or getting too chilly.

Shallow water is best. Birds like to wade, but they don't like to swim. Therefore, choose a bath 2 to 3 inches deep, with sides that slope gradually. The ideal diameter is 24 to 36 inches.

Keep it clean. Add fresh water frequently. If the bath gets dirty or mossy, scrub it with a brush, empty it out, and fill it with fresh water.

Circulate the water. The sound of splashing water attracts birds. You can create a fountain and recirculate the water by adding a small submersible pump with a spray head.

Foil predators. Place elevated birdbaths near trees or shrubs to provide birds with quick escape routes. Place ground-level baths in spots with 10 to 20 feet of open space on all sides. Any less space leaves birds open to cat ambush; any more makes them perfect targets for owls and hawks.

Stones

Stones are natural and timeless. They give a sense of permanence to any garden. Unfortunately, they're never around where you need them. A gathering of large stones in an area where you want a small lawn is no help at all. Neither is that gorgeous boulder that's blocking the view of your garden beyond.

But not to worry. All it takes is a strong back and maybe some heavy equipment to place those stones exactly where you want them. You can create rock gardens, walls, and steps in a matter of days, and build stone benches and sculptures in just a few hours. If your garden lacks stones of any real consequence, consult a local quarry or stone supplier. They can fix you up with everything from gravel and flagstones to massive boulders.

Before you buy, consider your site. Are water-washed granite boulders appropriate to your region? Or might slabs of slate look best? Whatever type of stone you choose, think twice before you act. You won't want to move a 2-ton boulder more than once.

Gathering Moss

A rolling stone gathers no moss, but a secure, established one does. Moss is the garden's patina that naturally takes months to develop. But if you want that green carpet sooner, you can speed up the process. Try this special moss-accelerating formula on newly placed stones and statues.

First, stir a fist-size lump of porcelain clay (available at craft shops or ceramic supply companies) into 3 cups of water until the mixture has the consistency of a thick milk shake. Then combine the clay suspension with 1 cup of undiluted liquid fish fertilizer and 1 cup of fresh, shredded moss. Whisk the mixture thoroughly, then paint it on your stones and statues with a brush. As you paint, remember that moss grows naturally in patches, favors the north side of any object, and takes readily to crevices. If you apply this formula in a moist and shady location, you may well have moss in a matter of weeks.

Garden of Stone

This Japanese-style garden is a well-planned composition. Its beauty is in its simplicity. Its sculpted grace, a quiet sanctuary that calms the mind while heightening the senses.

The raked gravel suggests rippling water that follows the outline of the stone-carved island. The sculpture reaches skyward, while a small reflecting pool brings a piece of the sky down to Earth. The water also provides movement when the wind creates a current on its surface.

A special wooden rake is used to create the pattern in the gravel. To establish the desired flow, walk backwards while pulling the rake firmly through the gravel. When finished, set the resulting "waves" with a fine spray of water.

Consider installing a gravel path to connect a garden such as this with other landscape vignettes or thematic garden areas.

ABOVE *Chunky boulders, smooth river stones, and squared-off stone slabs fit right into this gentle slope, adding an impressive architectural element to the garden.*

Furniture

Whether made of wood, metal, or stone, an outdoor chair or bench offers a welcome respite where you can sit a while, relax, and enjoy the view. It can also be the finishing touch that completes a garden retreat.

Consider the garden setting and style before you select furniture. In a formal garden, for example, a rustic willow chair might look out of place; wrought

INSET BELOW *An inviting hammock-chair is suspended from a sturdy oak crossbar. The plump cushions are covered in washable acrylic.*

BOTTOM *A group of wicker rocking chairs graces this screened porch, where insect pests are kept out while cooling breezes are welcomed in.*

iron chairs and a table in the Victorian style, however, could be perfect. Some chairs are quite comfortable but not very attractive. Some good-looking benches are hard on the back.

Try out different kinds of chairs and benches at an outdoor-furniture store before you buy or build your own. Just like Goldilocks in search of the perfect fit, you'll find one that's just right for you.

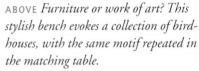

ABOVE *Furniture or work of art? This stylish bench evokes a collection of bird-houses, with the same motif repeated in the matching table.*

LEFT *The natural patina of wood furniture is in perfect harmony with the warm tones of a brick patio.*

BELOW LEFT *This antique dining set, protected from rain and sun by the porch roof, makes outdoor meals an everyday treat.*

BELOW RIGHT *Weathered Adirondack chairs in a "woodland" of ferns, hostas, and azaleas offer the promise of cool relief from hot afternoons.*

Benches

Of the outdoor furniture set, benches tend to be appreciated more for their good looks and style than their easy comfort and practicality. It makes sense, then, to consider them for their beauty and "fit" with your garden style.

Keep in mind that the location of a bench should be plausible, accessible, and pleasant. (A bench next to a path makes sense; one in a thicket doesn't.) A bench in the distance can draw visitors through your garden and lead them to a pretty view, while a bench beneath an arbor or a leafy bough *is* the view.

In choosing the type of bench you want, think of the setting and the amount of maintenance the material it's made of requires. Cast iron looks wonderful in old-style gardens but may require occasional painting. Woods such as pine or oak will need a good sealer or periodic paint. Teak, aluminum, stone, and concrete can withstand decades of heavy weather without fuss or bother. And don't forget about benches made of synthetic wicker. This durable material may look and feel like natural wicker (a less sturdy material better suited to sheltered areas), but it is unaffected by weather and doesn't sag or rot when wet.

TOP *Curvaceous fronds of an ornate fern are indelibly captured in cast iron.*

ABOVE *A stylish bench and flower garden create an enchanting retreat in a front courtyard.*

LEFT *Extended from a garden wall, this shelf of stone offers a place to linger.*

LEFT *An elegant Lutyens bench, painted in fresh white, is perfectly placed among banks of blue hydrangeas.*

TOP *Though spotlighted by late afternoon light, this bench is shaded from midday sun by the boughs of a larch* (Larix).

ABOVE *Handsome supports and a marble top make this classic bench as much a garden sculpture as a convenient place to sit.*

Hideaway Storage

Tired of looking at that unattractive hose in the lovely garden you've created? Hide it away in a handsome storage bench. You can place the bench in the garden, next to

the back door, or just outside a shed to hold small tools, rubber boots, and gloves, as well.

A good bench withstands the elements, so galvanized hinges and screws are important. As for wood, consider using the stars of rot resistance—cypress, cedar, redwood, or teak. If you choose teak, you won't need marine varnish or an exterior stain. For the other woods, you will. In all cases, brush the bench or spray it with the hose to remove dust and dirt.

Garden Art

A garden is like a stage populated with performers. You can keep the cast simple by staying with the mainstream stars—trees, shrubs, flowers, and lawn—but, sometimes, it's the character actors that make a performance sparkle. In the garden, these players are collectively known as "garden art."

To find or create garden art requires nothing more than a little imagination. Often the perfect accent is something typically used for a more utilitarian purpose, or an object salvaged from an uncertain fate. Put an old wheelbarrow to use, for example, by filling it with potting soil and planting it with seasonal annuals.

Take bits of ironwork and architectural fragments and turn them into pieces of sculpture—or use old garden implements (such as hoes and scythes) to adorn a garden wall or fence. Something as quick and easy as a coat of bright paint (see page 211) can change a tired old chair into a whimsical focal point.

Beyond your garage or attic you'll find a world of accent possibilities. Garage sales and salvage yards are good places to look for eclectic sculptural pieces for little cost. If your garden's style calls for something a bit more upscale, specialty shops and outdoor sculpture galleries are logical venues for statuary, fountains, sundials, jardinieres, and sundry other items. Mail-order catalogs also offer a wide assortment of garden-art pieces such as sculptures, wall plaques, metal art, and colorful containers and urns.

TOP LEFT *This cast-iron weather vane is painted to look like aged copper.*

TOP RIGHT *Energy seems to emanate from the hub and spokes of this sun-gold iron wheel.*

RIGHT *Pairs of Corinthian columns lead the eye to a focal point of classical statuary.*

TOP LEFT *Frozen in mime: a concrete rooster crows from his perch behind a flowering clematis.*

TOP CENTER *A weatherproofed picture frame creates a portrait of the distant meadow.*

TOP RIGHT *Look again. The marsh bird and cattails are a metal sculpture nestled among clumps of ornamental grass.*

ABOVE *Hare today… and tomorrow, this concrete rabbit stands watch over a garden path.*

LEFT *Commanding attention, a wooden obelisk rises like a medieval tower from a bed of roses.*

RIGHT *Appropriately recycled, an aging wheelbarrow gains new life as a rustic container for colorful annuals.*

INSET BELOW *Curls of wrought iron offer a perfect support for the vining stems of anemone clematis (Clematis montana).*

BOTTOM *A simple, unadorned jardiniere makes an understated centerpiece in a garden of diverse foliage colors and textures.*

Display Basics

A successful display of garden art depends on more than just the object itself. Keep in mind the following suggestions when creating your design.

Punctuate Your Garden

If your garden lacks a focal point, give it one—a sculpture, statue, fountain, or other object that cannot be ignored. A dark, plain background such as hedges or evergreen shrubs will help the focal point shine; an arbor in front creates an excellent frame for viewing.

Consider Size and Scale

A large sculpture might overwhelm a small garden, while a small piece might look lost in lush foliage. To prevent ▶

ABOVE *An antique angel pays perpetual homage to a planting of Lenten roses* (Helleborus orientalis).

RIGHT *Secured atop a classic pedestal, this gazing ball reflects the image of a lovely bench.*

ABOVE *Sparkling in brilliant color, this glamorous mosaic tortoise dresses up a lush bed of chartreuse-leafed dead nettle* (Lamium maculatum 'Chequers').

RIGHT *Cast concrete decorative pieces in Colonial-era fashion complement formal gardens in period style.*

Finishing Touches

such problems, place pieces in various parts of the yard until you find spots that suit each perfectly.

Choose a Style

Combining styles—classic antiquity and contemporary abstract, for example—is risky, especially if artistic accents will appear close to one another. You're more likely to create a pleasing picture if you decide on one artistic style and stick with it. Avoid over-accessorizing your garden: it will just seem cluttered. You can always add more accents later.

TOP *Held aloft by a bronze figure, an armillary sphere adds a touch of celestial antiquity to the surrounding garden.*

ABOVE *On the job in any weather, this angular metal man is the garden's permanent welcoming committee of one.*

LEFT *An assertive red chair is functional garden art, its eye-commanding color repeated in the decorative gazing globes and the foreground foliage.*

LEFT *A garden chair in eccentric style draws even more attention thanks to a coat of periwinkle blue paint.*

BELOW *Painted in elaborate patterns, these terra-cotta pots and wooden planter are works of art.*

Paint

Color can spotlight any part of a garden, and one of the simplest ways to add color is with paint. We're not suggesting the Queen of Hearts' approach of painting all the roses red, but a brightly colored wall, door, or gate, for example, can create an immediate focal point. Take advantage of paint's transforming ability with smaller objects, too: painting an old chair, a fanciful birdhouse, or plain terra-cotta pots can add a magical touch in any garden.

Paint Pointers

To achieve the best finish, paint in fair weather, out of direct sun, after morning dew, and at least 2 hours before evening dampness arrives. Prepare the surface by removing dirt, grease, rust, and paint flakes.

For new wood, prime the surface with one or two coats of latex or exterior wood primer. Then paint with flat latex acrylic, vinyl exterior enamel, or house paint in the desired finish.

For plaster and stucco, use exterior latex or acrylic paint. A roller will give more uniform coverage.

For cast-iron furniture, remove every speck of rust (using steel wool, sanding blocks, or a rust-removing substance will do it); then coat with a rust-resistant paint.

Lighting

Lighting can dramatically
change the look of a
garden, softening lines and
edges and highlighting patterns and textures in its glow.
It serves a practical purpose,
too: well-placed lamps can
guide visitors.

Good lighting begins with
a plan. Before installing fixtures, think of the effect you
want to achieve. Lights near a
window can draw the eye outside,
effectively enlarging the indoors
and easing the transition between
home and garden. A light mounted
high in a tree can cast a pool of
"moonlight" on the ground.
Strands of twinkle lights under a
patio roof or arbor can transform
an evening outdoors into a fiesta.

You can achieve many interesting effects through the creative use
of lighting, such as illuminating
sculptural trunks and branches,
spotlighting garden art, and projecting plant silhouettes onto
walls. In most gardens, low-voltage
systems will do the trick. They're
easy to install and easy to adjust,
and they use less energy than
standard-current fixtures.

INSET ABOVE *Like a jar of glowing
fireflies, a tin lantern filled with clear
holiday lights adds a welcoming note
to an entry.*

RIGHT *Handsome path lights bathe
garden beds in gold, and illuminate
the walkway and steps for safe passage.*

BELOW *Uplighting from well-placed spotlights transforms these trunks into radiant sculptures.*

BOTTOM *Isn't it romantic? Strings of holiday lights laced through wisteria provide an alluring glow overhead.*

Lighting Effects

Some outdoor lights—such as lanterns, path lights, and wall-mounted units—are made to be seen; most, however, are meant to blend in the background. For this reason, be sure to hide the fixtures as well as you can, and aim them so that the light bulbs are shielded from direct view. The idea is to make your garden—not your lights—the star of the show.

Backlighting gives lacy shrubs a delicate glow.

Path lights can edge walks or shine down from eaves.

Sidelighting dense plants defines shape and detail.

Shadowing casts plant silhouettes against walls.

"Moonlighting" creates soft pools of light.

"Grazing" showcases structure and texture.

Uplighting reveals form and canopy of trees.

Standard Current or Low Voltage?

Outdoor lights can be powered by standard house-hold current or by low-voltage systems. Each method has its advantages and drawbacks.

Standard current. For large gardens or those still in the planning stage, standard systems work well. These systems tend to last longer than low-voltage systems, and they cast strong light into tall trees. On the other hand, standard systems tend to be more expensive, more difficult to move, and harder to aim and conceal.

RIGHT *An octagonal umbrella casts cooling shade by day and charming light by night.*

BELOW *Tubes of tiny lights along a trellis add subtle sparkle above, while a hidden spotlight creates drama below.*

The installation alone can be daunting. You'll need to get a building permit, wire all circuits through ground-fault circuit interrupters, and encase all wires in rigid conduit—unless you bury them at least 18 inches deep.

Low voltage. For smaller areas or established gardens that you don't want to upset with lots of digging, consider a low-voltage system. These lights, which use transformers that reduce household current to 12 volts, consume less energy and are easier to install than standard fixtures. They're also safer, more portable, and easier to aim. On the downside, the number of lamps that can be attached to one transformer is limited. Always choose high-quality metal fixtures. They cost more than plastic fixtures but last longer and look much better.

Candles

As a candle flame dances and flickers, sparkles and glows, it creates an alluring, almost hypnotic effect. Perhaps this is why we seem to relax in the primitive pleasure of firelight.

Before setting out those candles, however, keep in mind a few basics. First, nearly any candle will smoke or drip if it's placed in a draft. So shield it inside a paper sack with sand in the bottom or in a hurricane lamp, a glass jar, or even a tin can with artfully punched holes in the sides. Next, locate candles where they're not likely to be accidentally knocked over, come into contact with loose clothing, or damage nearby plants with their heat.

TOP LEFT *Casually arranged votive candles atop metal stakes make it possible to enjoy this window garden day and night.*

ABOVE LEFT, INSET *Pumpkin-colored candles aligned on the mantle of an outdoor fireplace echo the color of autumn's signature fruit.*

ABOVE *An antique mold makes an unusual vessel for candles shaped like lotus blossoms.*

LEFT *A rustic candelabra casts soft light for intimate outdoor dining.*

Climate Zones of the South

IOW.

NEBRASKA

COLORADO

KANSAS

MISS

Denver

70

70

70

70

Arkansas River

25

Missouri River

Kansas City

Wichita

135

35

Springfield

44

13

MISS

Rio Grande River

Santa Fe

Upper
South

TEXAS

OKLAHOMA

Tulsa

35

44

Bosto
Mount

40

25

Albuquerque

Amarillo

40

Oklahoma
City

40

Arkansas River

Fort
Smith

Ouachita
Mountains

ARKAN

NEW MEXICO

27

Middle
South

44

35

Ouachita
Mountains

Roswell

Lubbock

Wichita
Falls

Lake
Texoma

30

Alamogordo

287

30

167

MEXICO

El Paso

10

10

10

Abilene

Midland
Odessa

20

20

Fort
Worth

Dallas

35

45

20

20

Lower
South

Shreveport

20

167

49

84

Al

Rio Grande River

Davis
Mountains

10

TEXAS

Waco

Lower
South

10

Austin

10

45

Lake
Charles

10

Coa
Sou

LOU

San
Antonio

35

Houston

45

37

Corpus
Christi

Gulf of
Mexico

Rio Grande R.

Coastal
South

Tropical
South

Brownsville

Average Annual Minimum Temperature

Temperature (°F)	Zone Color	
-20 to -1		Upper South
0 to 10		Middle South
11 to 20		Lower South
21 to 30		Coastal South
31 to 40		Tropical South

PENNSYLVANIA

INDIANA
OHIO
ILLINOIS

Pittsburgh
Philadelphia
Wilmington
Delaware Bay
Dover
DELAWARE

Wheeling
Columbus
Indianapolis
Cincinnati
Cumberland
Frederick
Baltimore
Washington, D.C.
Alexandria
MARYLAND
Chesapeake Bay

WEST
VIRGINIA
Appalachian Mountains

Charleston
Charlottesville
Richmond
VIRGINIA
Virginia Beach

Louis
Cape Girardeau
Paducah
Louisville
Lexington
KENTUCKY
Upper South
Appalachian Mountains
Lynchburg
Middle South
Winston-Salem
Durham
Lower South
Greensboro
Raleigh
Greenville

Bowling Green
Nashville
Knoxville
Asheville
Charlotte
NORTH CAROLINA
Wilmington

nesboro
TENNESSEE
Middle South
Chattanooga
Appalachian Mountains
Blue Ridge Mountains
Spartanburg
Greenville
Columbia
SOUTH CAROLINA
Florence
Charleston

Memphis
Huntsville
Atlanta
Augusta

ock
Tupelo
Gadsden
Birmingham
Anniston
Macon
Savannah

MISSISSIPPI
Columbus
Tuscaloosa
Columbus
ALABAMA
GEORGIA
Coastal South
Atlantic Ocean

Jackson
Meridian
Montgomery
Lower South
Albany
Okefenokee Swamp

Hattiesburg
Mobile
Dothan
Jacksonville

Baton Rouge
Biloxi
Pensacola
Tallahassee
Gainesville
Lake George
Daytona Beach

Lake Maurepas
Lake Pontchartrain
Lake Borgne
ANA
New Orleans
Mississippi R.
The Delta
Coastal South
Orlando

Tampa
FLORIDA

Gulf of Mexico
Lake Okeechobee
Fort Myers
Sanibel Island
Miami
The Everglades

0   50   100   150 Miles
Tropical South
Florida Keys
Key West

217

Subject Index

Index of Common and Botanical Names

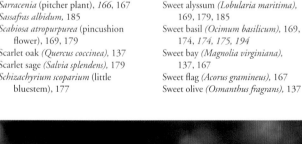

ACKNOWLEDGMENTS

A special thank you to Susan Bryan of the Joseph W. Jones Ecological Research Center at Ichauway in Newton, Georgia; Carrie Dodson Davis; Fiona Gilsenan; Danielle Javier; Lyngso Garden Materials; Audrey Mak; Christine Rocha; Richard M. Shapiro; Smith & Hawken; Trex, Inc.; and Patti Zeman.

We also thank the writers, editors, artists, designers, and consultants who contributed to the development of previous editions of landscaping books published by Oxmoor House, Inc., and Sunset Publishing Corporation. Much of their work lives on in this edition.

PHOTOGRAPHY CREDITS

Unless otherwise noted, photographs are courtesy of Southern Progress Corporation Photo Collection, which includes the work of Jean Allsopp, Ralph Anderson, Van Chaplin, Tina Cornett, Sylvia Martin, Art Meripol, Allen Rokach, and Laurey Weigant.

Each image is identified by its page number and position on the page. Vertical positions are top (T), middle (M), and bottom (B); horizontal positions are left (L), center (C), and right (R).

Jean Allsopp: 142 B; 179 B; 191 TR, BR. Ralph Anderson: 28–29 all; 36–37 all; 215 R; 223. Arena Roses: 149 TL. David Belda: 193 TR. Mark Bolton/Garden Image: 192 TL. Paul Bousquet: 173 TL. Marion Brenner: 118; 129 TR. Kathleen Brenzel: 199 MC. Judith Bromley: 159 BL. Gay Bumgarner: 160 B; 178 BR; 203 TL. Karen Bussolini: 96 BL; 159 MR; 159 TR. Ed Carey: 193 TL. David Cavagnaro: 155 MR; 160 T; 161 TL; 163 TL. Walter Chandoha: 109 BR. Van Chaplin: 2 L; 5 TR; 40–43 all; 70 T; 71 T; 76 BL; 140; 166 L, BC; BR; 167 MR, BR; 184 all; 188–189; 192 BR; 210 BL; 215 ML; 218 B; 219. Peter Christiansen: 199 TC. Gary Clark: 209 BR. Rosalind Creasy: 172 T; 173. Claire Curran: 144 B. Robin Bachtler Cushman: 178 TL. Dalton Pavilion, Inc: 95 L. Janet Davis: 213 BL. R. Todd Davis: 156 R. Alan & Linda Detrick: 182 BR. Andrew Drake: 209 BL. Ken Druse: 4 TR; 80–81; 168 BR. Colleen Duffley: 93 B. Catriona Tudor Erler: 114 B. Derek Fell: 183 TR. Scott Fitzgerrell: 85 B. Roger Foley: 67 BR; 205 TR (design by Guy Williams); 208 TR. Frank Gaglione: 102 T, B; 123 TL, BL, BR; 124 B. Tria Giovan: 202 B. John Glover: 77 B. Steven Gunther: 70 B;

71 B. Mick Hales: 205 MR. Jerry Harpur: 54 T; 157 TL; 167 TL; 211 T. Lynne Harrison: 200 B. Philip Harvey: 56 B; 78 L; 83 B; 89 B; 107 BL; 202 T; 214 BR. H. Ross Hawkins: 178 T. Alex Hayden: 101 all. Saxon Holt: 125 T; 145 B; 146 M; 149 BR; 149 TR; 164 all; 186 B. Mary Gray Hunter: 153 MR; 176; 177 L, ML, R; 185 T. Jean-Claude Hurni (design by Jean-Claude Hurni & Rêve-Rives): 127 T. Dency Kane: 159 BR; 172–173 B; 210 TR. Andrew Lawson: 154 L. Susanne Loosmoore: 158 B; 161 TR. Janet Loughrey: 141 B (design by Francine Day, Tom Zachary Landscape Architects); 157 TR; 179 T; 208 B. Allan Mandell: 147 B; 201. Charles Mann: 82 T (design by Greg Trutza); 155 ML; 165 BL. Sylvia Martin: 76 T. Maslowski Wildlife Productions: 199 ML, TR. Mayer/LeScanff, The Garden Picture Library: 166 TR. Jack McDowell: 106 B. E. Andrew McKinney: 123 TR; 203 TR, 209 BC (design by Erick Cortina/Roger's Gardens). Nightscaping: 213 TL. Katie O'Hara-Kelly: 173 TR. Jerry Pavia: 147 T; 148 TC; 149 BL; 159 ML, TL; 161 B; 165 TL; 177 MR; 183 BR; 199 TL. Norm Plate: 199 BC. Norman A. Plate: 60 T; 61 TL; 79 L; 79 R; 102 M; 119; 138 T; 192 TR, BL;

193 BL; 211 R. Ian Reeves: 61 B. Cheryl Richter: 135; 159 TC. Allen Rokach: 5 TL; 8–11 all; 71 M; 130–131. Susan A. Roth: 178 MR; 182 TL; 203 BR. Jim Sadlon: 214 TR. Lauren Springer: 69 TL. Thomas J. Story: 78 R; 79 C; 190 BR; 193 BR. Michael S. Thompson: 99 TR; 148 BR; 149 TC; 171 R; 200 T. Trex, Inc.: 97 R. Jessie Walker: 66 B. Deidra Walpole: 207 TC. judywhite/GardenPhotos.com: 100. Peter O. Whiteley: 94 T; 103 B. Tom Woodward: 4 ML; 5 B; 137 T. Cynthia Woodyard: 166 MC. Ben Woolsey: 67 TR. Tom Wyatt: 60 B (all); 75 TL.

ILLUSTRATION CREDITS

Beverley Bozarth Colgan, Deborah Cowder, Peter Eckert, Tracy La Rue Hohn, Lois Lovejoy, Rik Olson, Mimi Osborne, Reineck & Reineck, Wendy Smith, Jenny Speckels, Elisa Tanaka.